God through Cosmic Lenses

God through Cosmic Lenses

Quantum Mystery and Infinite Personality

VICTOR FOLKERT

WIPF & STOCK · Eugene, Oregon

GOD THROUGH COSMIC LENSES
Quantum Mystery and Infinite Personality

Copyright © 2022 Victor Folkert. All rights reserved. Except for brief quotations in critical publications or reviews, no part of this book may be reproduced in any manner without prior written permission from the publisher. Write: Permissions, Wipf and Stock Publishers, 199 W. 8th Ave., Suite 3, Eugene, OR 97401.

Wipf & Stock
An Imprint of Wipf and Stock Publishers
199 W. 8th Ave., Suite 3
Eugene, OR 97401

www.wipfandstock.com

PAPERBACK ISBN: 978-1-6667-4192-6
HARDCOVER ISBN: 978-1-6667-4193-3
EBOOK ISBN: 978-1-6667-4194-0

08/26/22

Scriptures taken from the Holy Bible, New International Version®, NIV®. Copyright © 1973, 1978, 1984, 2011 by Biblica, Inc.™ Used by permission of Zondervan. All rights reserved worldwide. www.zondervan.com The "NIV" and "New International Version" are trademarks registered in the United States Patent and Trademark Office by Biblica, Inc.™

Contents

Introduction | 1

Deep | 8
Near | 20
Always | 34
Infinite | 48
Personal | 61
Infinitely Personal | 93
With Us | 109
For Us | 125
More | 151

Bibliography | 165

Introduction

> Imagination is more important than knowledge. Knowledge is limited. Imagination encircles the world.[1]
>
> —Albert Einstein

> That night my imagination was, in a certain sense, baptized.[2]
>
> —C.S. Lewis

BOTH SCIENCE AND FAITH require imagination—not the kind of imagination that avoids reality, but the kind that explores reality.

My three-year-old granddaughter imagines a cat living in her closet. It works for her: she can be happy about the cat, and she doesn't have to feed it or empty the litter box. She can give a name to her cat and even imagine how it acts and feels, but someday her imaginary cat will disappear, because it exists only in her imagination.

My granddaughter also imagines her grandfather. I am quite real, but her image of me is limited, since she only sees me once or twice a year, and never in my office or on the basketball court. In her three-year-old mind, she cannot comprehend my deepest thoughts or rawest emotions. Yet in her imagination, she embraces what she knows of me and lays a foundation for knowing me better as she grows and we spend more time together.

1. Nilsson, "Albert Einstein: Imagination."
2. Lewis, *Surprised by Joy*, 181.

Imagination is a useful tool for exploring reality—even the unseen realities of God and the universe.

IMAGINING PHYSICAL REALITY

> It is surprising that people do not believe that there is imagination in science. It is a very interesting kind of imagination, unlike that of the artist. The great difficulty is in trying to imagine something that you have never seen, that is consistent in every detail with what has already been seen, and that is different from what has been thought of; furthermore, it must be definite and not a vague proposition. That is indeed difficult.[3]
>
> —RICHARD P. FEYNMAN

Reality transcends human comprehension.

In high school chemistry, students learn about the Bohr model of the atom. The model gives a simple picture of an atom, with a nucleus consisting of positively charged protons and uncharged neutrons, surrounded by negatively charged electrons at increasing energy levels outside the nucleus.

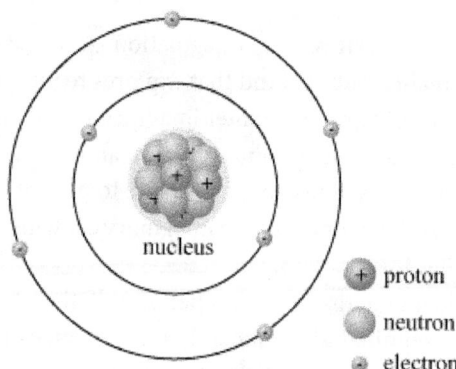

The Bohr model is elegant and useful in visualizing atoms and molecular bonding. It can be misleading, however, as it pictures electrons as little balls orbiting a spherical nucleus, like planets orbiting the sun. In reality, electrons are not little balls, and they do not occupy circles around the

---

3. Feynman, *Meaning of It All*, 22–23.

nucleus. In fact, it is impossible to precisely determine their position and momentum at any given time.

Scientific models are ways of imagining deeper reality. They are useful to the extent they are consistent with observation, and they can be modified or superseded, based on new discoveries or understanding.

Re-Imagining Physical Reality

> While it is never safe to affirm that the future of Physical Science has no marvels in store even more astonishing than those of the past, it seems probable that most of the grand underlying principles have been firmly established, and that further advances are to be sought chiefly in the rigorous applications of these principles to all the phenomena which come under our notice. It is here that the science of measurement shows its importance...[4]
>
> —A.A. MICHELSON, 1894

Michelson was the first American physicist to win a Nobel Prize. Ironically, although he thought few great underlying principles were still to be discovered, his measurement of the speed of light as a fundamental constant was foundational for Einstein's groundbreaking Theory of Special Relativity.

By the time Michelson died in 1933, physics had been turned upside down. Space and time were joined in a theory of relativity, and gravity was viewed as curvature of space-time. Mass and energy were linked through Einstein's famous equation, $E=mc^2$. Quantum mechanics emerged as a fundamental principle.

Twentieth-century developments in physics further challenged perceptions of the universe. On the large scale of astrophysics, scientists discovered quasars and black holes, cosmic background radiation, and an expanding universe. On the opposite end of the scale, they encountered deep mysteries of quantum vacuums, entanglement, and superposition.

New discoveries caused physicists to reframe the laws of nature. They imagined quantum reality in terms of uncertainty, probability amplitudes, potentialities, model-dependent realism, and measurement-created events.

Such concepts might sound strange to those not familiar with physics, and explanations will follow in future chapters. The strangeness will not

---

4. Michelson, *Annual Register 1894–1895*, 150.

disappear, however, for reality challenges the limits of the human mind. As a quote falsely attributed to Einstein says, "Once you can accept the universe as matter expanding into nothing that is something, wearing stripes with plaid comes easily."

Although quantum physics blossomed in the early twentieth century, its implications are just beginning to make their way into the worldview of many people.

IMAGINING GOD

> (God) sits enthroned above the circle of the earth, and its
> people are like grasshoppers. He stretches out the heavens
> like a canopy, and spreads them out like a tent to live in.
>
> —Isaiah 40:22

> Who is so devoid of intellect as not to understand that
> God, in so speaking, lisps with us as nurses are wont to do
> with little children? Such modes of expression, therefore,
> do not so much express what kind of a being God is, as
> accommodate the knowledge of him to our feebleness.[5]
>
> —John Calvin

If the mysteries of the natural world exceed human comprehension, the mysteries of God are even more impenetrable. Human comprehension is limited by the boundaries of the universe, the time span of human awareness, and the development of human minds. God transcends those boundaries.

The writers of the Bible imagined God, whom they could not fully comprehend, in the framework of their experience. Isaiah imagined God stretching out the heavens like a tent. Moses spoke of seeing God's back, but not his face.[6] David imagined God as a shepherd, guiding and protecting him.[7] Jesus told parables that invited his hearers to imagine God as a father, a master of a household, or a rich man inviting street people to enjoy his banquet.

---

5. John Calvin, *Institutes of the Christian Religion*, I, 13, 1.
6. Exod 33:18–23.
7. Psalm 23.

Introduction

Imagination can lead people astray, however. History teems with gods as projections of human thoughts or experiences: supernatural humans, animals embodying traits of strength or sexuality, or abstract human ideals such as wisdom or beauty. God warned his people not to worship any image of him, because human-created images can never capture the deep reality of God himself.

Although few people today worship physical images, all people—even those who don't believe he exists—have mental images of God. Some reflect his essential nature, while others might be misleading or shallow.

Childish Images of God

> When I was a child, I talked like a child, I thought
> like a child, I reasoned like a child. When I became a
> man, I put the ways of childhood behind me.
>
> —1 CORINTHIANS 13:11

A child might imagine God as a stern father who punishes disobedience. He might think of God as an indulgent grandfather, who grants every wish. He might think God lives in a church building or a far-off heaven.

Images of God that develop during childhood sometimes persist into adulthood, when of course they prove inadequate for an adult view of the world.

Secondhand Images of God

Some people imagine God in the image of a parent, a grandparent, or a respected pastor or youth leader. Those raised in a strict church or religious school might think of God as a rule-enforcer. Those who have heard only about God's love might think of him as their rich benefactor.

Secondhand images eventually prove inadequate. The faith of a godly grandmother might seem shallow in an academic environment. A God of prosperity might be deeply disappointing when a job is lost or a business fails. Simple rules of conduct might be ineffective in a complex political or social environment.

God through Cosmic Lenses

Culturally-Biased Images of God

Imagination is shaped by media, politics, education, and social groups.

In a culture where many are "spiritual but not religious," God might be imagined as a mystical sensation or a bright light. In an anxious environment, he might be felt as a comforting touch. In a twelve-step group, he is a higher power. For a sentimental soul, he might be surrounded by cherubic angels and an aura of love.

In a culture that values tolerance above all else, people might imagine God as lenient and indulgent, while those troubled by cultural decay might imagine that God hates the same people they do. Prosperous Americans might imagine God as fair-minded and rewarding hard work, while people who endure oppression might think of him as a defender of justice, powerful in the face of evil.

Outdated Images of God

> (Older adolescents were asked around 1950), "Do you think God understands radar?" In nearly every case the answer was no, followed of course by a laugh, as the conscious mind realized the absurdity of the answer.[8]
>
> —J.B. Phillips

Although radar had been developed in the 1930s, the young people had never considered that God would understand the behavior of electromagnetic waves in the universe he created.

Popular imagination of God often lags behind scientific knowledge. For example, although the immensity of the universe was known from the second century onward,[9] some people still imagine God to be "up in the clouds somewhere."

---

8. Phillips, *Your God Is Too Small*, 20.

9. C.S. Lewis quotes Ptolemy's *Almagest*, which was the standard astronomical handbook from the second century into the Middle Ages. Lewis, "Religion and Science," 74.

Introduction

Re-Imagining God

> [God's] essence, indeed, is incomprehensible, utterly transcending all human thought; but on each of his works his glory is engraved... In attestation of his wondrous wisdom, both the heavens and the earth present us with innumerable proofs... which astronomy, medicine, and all the natural science are designed to illustrate... those who are more or less intimately acquainted with those liberal studies are thereby assisted and enabled to obtain a deeper insight into the secret workings of divine wisdom.[10]
>
> —JOHN CALVIN, AD 1536

Calvin recognized that God transcends human comprehension, and he endorsed science as a means of revealing God's glory in the beauty and grandeur of the universe. He looked to scientists—"those acquainted with liberal studies"—to give deeper insight into the mysteries of God.

As classical science advanced, it constructed a conceptual framework of definitions and natural laws. Classical theology followed a similar course, distilling the facts and mysteries of God into propositional statements defining essential truths. The *Westminster Larger Catechism* of 1647 answered the question, "What [!] is God?" with, "God is a Spirit, in and of himself infinite in being, glory, blessedness, and perfection; all-sufficient, eternal, unchangeable, incomprehensible, everywhere present, almighty, knowing all things, most wise, most holy, most just, most merciful and gracious, longsuffering, and abundant in goodness and truth."[11]

Scientific advances in the past century have yielded new discoveries and understanding, as well as new models for imagining the hidden workings of the universe. These scientific discoveries and models suggest new paradigms for imagining and exploring the mysteries of God.

---

10. Calvin, *Institutes of the Christian Religion*, I, 5, 1-2. Calvin saw no conflict between science and religion, although in the nineteenth century, F.W. Farrar falsely credited Calvin with the statement, "Who will place the authority of Copernicus above that of the Holy Spirit?" Calvin, with Augustine before him, allowed that new understandings of the natural world might cause traditional interpretations of Scripture to be reconsidered. Polkinghorne, *Science and the Trinity*, 2-3.

11 *Westminster Larger Catechism*, Q. 7.

Deep

> The sea is not the sea, if you can hold it in a spoon.[1]
>
> —Puritan Pastor Richard Baxter

IN THE ANCIENT STORY of the blind men and the elephant, six blind men try to determine what an elephant is like, by feeling different parts of its body. The man who feels a leg says the elephant is like a pillar. The one who feels the tail says it is like a rope. The one who feels the trunk says it is like a tree branch. The one who feels the ear says it is like a hand fan. The one who feels the belly says it is like a wall. The one who feels the tusk says it is like a solid pipe.

1. Baxter, "Divine Life," 29.

Deep

Varying implications have been drawn from the story. Some suggest that all points of view are equally valid. Others emphasize the value of shared perspectives and communication. Others argue that all religions have the same God, seen differently through different lenses.

Clearly, however, the elephant is not a fish or an airplane. The elephant is not imaginary. The elephant is not whatever people happen to think an elephant might be. There really is an elephant!

Humans perceive God through lenses of the created universe, history, and personal encounters. They integrate their perspectives to create a picture of God that fits into their minds, using logic, theology, and speculation. Yet human images can never capture the depth of God.

Let's turn the story around. Six elephants are discussing what humans are like. Since none of them has ever seen a human, they decide humans must be flat, like a picture one of them saw. Suddenly a man appears on the road in front of them. Horrified by his appearance, they charge at him, determining that he is, in fact, flat.

Just as elephants do not have the capacity to comprehend the intellectual, social, or psychological complexities of humans, humans do not have the capacity to comprehend God fully. Images that "flatten" God to fit human conceptions yield a distorted picture of God.

The deepest perceptions of God leave room for profound, even impenetrable mysteries. In the words of the apostle Paul in Romans 11:33, "Oh, the depth of the riches of the wisdom and knowledge of God! How unsearchable his judgments, and his paths beyond tracing out!"

As it turns out, the deepest perceptions of the universe also recognize profound, even impenetrable mysteries.

PARADOX AND MYSTERY

> How wonderful that we have met with a paradox.
> Now we have some hope of making progress.[2]
>
> —Niels Bohr

A paradox can be defined as an apparent contradiction between two statements or facts, both based on truth.

The story of the blind men and the elephant is a kind of paradox. The perspectives of the blind men seem contradictory, but all reflect accurate

---

2. Moore, *Niels Bohr*, 196.

observations. The apparent contradictions can be resolved by understanding that the blind men are touching different parts of the same animal.

Some paradoxes play upon word definitions. A statement like, "Deep down, you're really shallow," probes multiple meanings of "deep" and "shallow." Other paradoxes point to deeper truths. William Wordsworth's poetic line, "Child is father of the man," invites thoughtful reflection on how early experiences impact adults. George Orwell's statement in *Animal Farm*, "All animals are equal, but some are more equal than others," is profoundly relevant to economics, government, or education.[3]

Instead of attempting to resolve a paradox, it is sometimes better to explore deeper mysteries. An example is, "Diamonds are more valuable than water; yet water is worth more than diamonds." The paradox can be resolved by observing that value depends on one's perspective. In a desert where clean water is scarce, nothing is more valuable. At a wedding with plenty to drink, the diamond is of greater value. Paradox resolved!

The paradox raises deeper questions, however: Is survival the highest value, or is beauty of equal importance? Why do people value rare diamonds if they are of no practical value? If diamonds symbolize love and commitment, why do humans place such high value on those relationships?

Some scientific paradoxes can be resolved by clearer definitions, careful logic, or experimentation. Other paradoxes point to deeper mysteries.

A Paradox of Light

3 Orwell, *Animal Farm*, 128.

Even a young child observes that if she stands in the sunlight, she can see her shadow. The explanation seems simple: A beam of light travels in a straight line from the sun to the wall, unless it is blocked by an opaque object.

Yet shadows are not so simple! If I stand close to a doorframe and look at my shadow on the carpet, the shadow of my head appears to reach out to touch the shadow of the opening. (No, it was not a bad hair day!) Although there is nothing between my head and the doorframe to block the sunbeams of light, they do not reach their target.

This rudimentary paradox of shadows indicates that light is not as simple as beams of light.

Is Light a Particle or Wave?

Competing theories of the nature of light emerged in the seventeenth century. Earlier philosophers had imagined light as particles, and Isaac Newton promoted an influential particle model of "corpuscles" of light. Other prominent scientists, including Rene Descartes, Robert Hooke, and Christiaan Huygens, found evidence for wavelike behavior.

In 1803, Thomas Young conducted an experiment demonstrating wave characteristics of light. In an updated form of the experiment, a coherent laser light shines through a narrow vertical slit in a thin plate onto another surface.

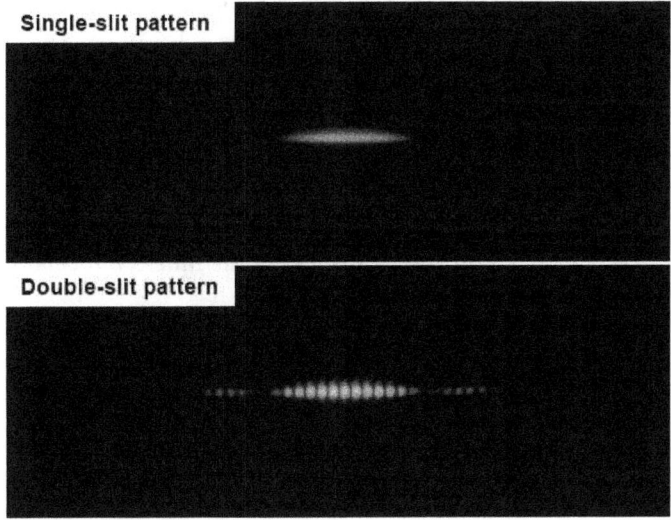

Jordgette, licensed under CC BY-SA 3.0

Intuitively, the idea of simple shadows implies that light will appear on the detector surface in the same narrow vertical pattern as the slit. Instead, light is diffracted horizontally, as shown in the single-slit pattern.

The diffraction is hard to explain in terms of particles, but it makes sense if light behaves like waves. Waves naturally spread from their source, like the wake of a boat on the water.

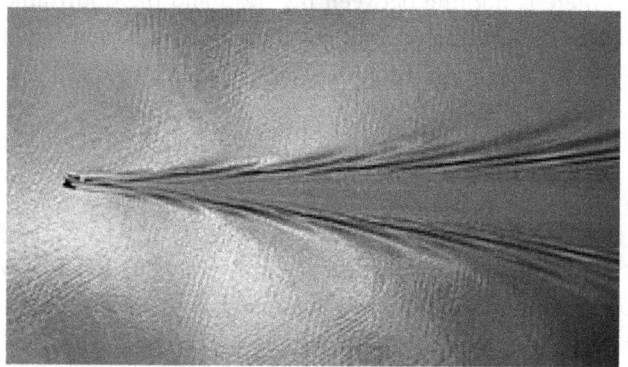

Boat sailing the Lyse Fjord in Norway by Edmont under CC BY-SA 3.0

A hypothesis that light acts like a wave is reinforced when there are two slits in the plate. Instead of two diffraction patterns on the detector, a single pattern of alternating light and dark areas emerges, as shown in the double-slit pattern above.

The pattern is consistent with the behavior of waves, which propagate from a source as alternating crests and troughs. When two crests or two troughs overlap, they reinforce each other, and when a crest overlaps a trough, they cancel each other out. As detectors are not at equal distances from each slit, the crests and troughs of the waves emanating from the slits will either reinforce or cancel each other.

A wave theory of light explains other phenomena as well, such as diffraction and polarization, and by the end of the nineteenth century, most scientists agreed that light consists of energy waves.

Paradoxical Pictures of Reality

> It seems as though we must use sometimes the one theory
> and sometimes the other, while at times we may use either.
> We are faced with a new kind of difficulty. We have two

Deep

contradictory pictures of reality; separately neither of them fully explains the phenomena of light, but together they do.[4]

—Albert Einstein

Einstein received the Nobel Prize in Physics in 1921, not for his theory of relativity, but for a 1905 paper on the photoelectric effect. His paper viewed light as discrete packets of energy: "When a light ray is spreading from a point, the energy is not distributed continuously over ever-increasing spaces, but consists of a finite number of energy quanta that are localized in points in space, move without dividing, and can be absorbed or generated only as a whole."[5]

Like particles, Einstein's "energy quanta" (later called photons) could be individually detected and counted. Yet Einstein could not deny the wavelike behavior of light, as demonstrated in Young's double slit experiment. He embraced both pictures of reality as a paradox, fully explaining the phenomena of light.

The paradoxical behavior of light points to deeper mysteries, however.

A Mystery of Light

[The double slit experiment is] a phenomenon which is impossible, absolutely impossible, to explain in any classical way, and which has in it the heart of quantum mechanics. In reality, it contains the only mystery. *We cannot make the mystery go away by "explaining" how it works.*[6]

—Richard Feynman

In a modern laboratory, the double slit experiment can be repeated, with a twist. Instead of a beam of light, photons are emitted one at a time, passing through one or more slits before being detected on a target surface.

Photons imagined as particles might act like bullets shot somewhat inaccurately through slots in a wall. A bullet that goes through one of the slots will hit a detector directly behind the slot, or perhaps bounce off an

---

4 Einstein and Infeld, *Evolution of Physics*, 263.

5 Einstein, *Collected Papers*, 86.

6. Feynman, *Feynman Lectures*, 1–1. Feynman's lecture on the double slit experiment also adds detectors at the slits, raising an additional mystery of the measurement problem.

edge and ricochet a little wider. With bullets, it does not matter whether there is one slot or two.

Image courtesy of M. Goldman, *Physics 2000*, University of Colorado at Boulder.

Photons do not act like bullets, however; they exhibit wavelike behavior. If the plate has only one slit, the photons diffuse to strike detectors in numbers corresponding to the behavior of waves emanating from the slit. If the plate has two slits, they are detected in numbers corresponding to a wave interference pattern.

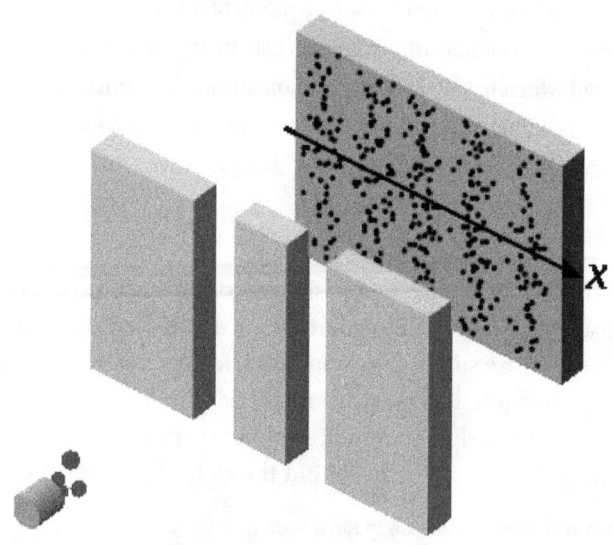

"File:Doubleslitexperiment.svg" by Koantum, svg version by Trutz Behn is licensed under CC BY-SA 3.0.

That is mystifying! The photons are emitted one at a time, and they travel from the emitter to detectors without interacting with other photons. Yet with two slits, they produce the same interference pattern as waves traveling through both slits!

What is happening? Does each photon morph into a wave, allowing it to go through both slits and create an interference pattern with itself? Does each photon have an imaginary twin that passes through the opposite slit? Is each photon surfing a hidden information wave that goes through both slits?

Answers to those questions are hidden in deep mysteries at the most fundamental level of the universe.

QUANTUM THEORY

> It is often stated that of all the theories proposed in this [twentieth] century, the silliest is quantum theory. Some say the only thing that quantum theory has going for it, in fact, is that it is unquestionably correct.[7]
>
> —RICHARD FEYNMAN

The origins of quantum physics can be traced to Max Planck, who demonstrated in 1900 that heated objects absorb or radiate energy only in discrete packets, which he called quanta. Einstein built on Planck's discovery in his 1905 paper on the photoelectric effect, using the term "quanta of light" to describe what came to be known as photons.

The scale of quantum physics is exceedingly tiny. Planck's formula for the energy of each discrete packet is $E = h\nu$, where ν is the frequency of the electromagnetic energy emitted, and h is 6.63×10^{-34} joule-seconds. Physicist Lisa Randall says that comparing a particle on that scale to a proton is about the same as comparing a proton to the state of Rhode Island.[8]

Photons as Quantum Particles.

When I power up my cell phone, tiny electrical pulses interact with the pixels of the screen to emit photons. Each photon carries a quantum packet of energy and momentum corresponding to the color frequency of the pixel.

---

7 Koku, *Hyperspace*, 262.

8. Randall, *Knocking on Heaven's Door*, 90.

Some of the photons strike receptors in my eye, and some illuminate the wall behind me.

Viewed as a particle, the location of a photon is elusive. As the photon emanates from a pixel, we might say it is "there." As it leaves the screen, it is "not there"—nowhere in particular, but potentially anywhere! If it reaches the back of my eye, it is "here"—not "there," and not "maybe somewhere else."

A non-quantum analogy is a cloud-based banking system. A customer deposits a twenty-dollar bill at an ATM, and the record of the balance disappears into "the cloud." If the customer logs onto an ATM on the network and receives a twenty dollar bill, the balance is no longer "somewhere in the cloud," but in his hand.

In the quantum world, however, the energy and momentum of the photon are not uniformly available. A photon from the screen of my phone is more likely to reach my eye than my wife's eye at the other end of the couch.

The potential locations where a photon might be detected correspond to a *probability wave function*. When a photon is emitted at the screen, it has a probability of "1" (100%) that it is "there." When it is no longer "there," the sum of the probabilities of detection across all possible locations is "1," with the probability at each location being "less than 1." If the photon is detected at any particular location, the probability wave function collapses to that location; the probability of the quantum of energy and momentum being "at that place" is "1," leaving zero probability of it being anywhere else.

Although the location is undetermined, it seems like the photon must be "somewhere" between "there" and "here," but that is impossible to prove! The only way to detect a photon "somewhere" is for the photon to interact with one or more quantum particles at that location. However, the interaction causes the photon to give up its energy and momentum, and the photon has zero probability of delivering the energy and momentum "here."

In a non-quantum analogy, a baseball follows a path from the pitcher's hand to the catcher's mitt. The path can be known without affecting the trajectory, because light or radar have insignificant impact on a baseball. Another baseball in the path, however, would disrupt the trajectory. In the case of a photon, no detector is smaller, and interaction with another particle obliterates the photon.

Yet what is the essence of a non-localized photon, whose probability of being anywhere in particular is less than 1? More simply, what is the reality of a photon that is potentially everywhere, nowhere in particular, but more likely to be found in some places than others?

Deep Quantum Mechanics

> Before Maxwell, Physical reality ... was thought of as consisting of material particles ... Since Maxwell's time, Physical Reality has been thought of as represented by continuous fields ...[9]
>
> —ALBERT EINSTEIN, 1931

Instead of viewing photons as particles with wave-like characteristics, quantum mechanics envisions photons as wave-like *fields* carrying quanta of energy and momentum.

Electromagnetic fields are everywhere around us. Radio waves convey a signal, microwaves warm food, and light illuminates the world. Yet fields are undetectable until they interact with something. A ray of light in a vacuum is unseen, and a radio wave is undetected until it interacts with a metal antenna.

Electromagnetic fields carry energy and momentum, and in the nineteenth century, James Clerk Maxwell condensed the behavior of those fields into four equations. Maxwell's equations are partial differential equations, which are essentially wave equations. Yet Einstein and others had discovered that the energy and momentum of electromagnetic fields are quantized: Radio or light waves comprise a large number of photons, each with a quantum of energy and momentum corresponding to the frequency of the wave.

In 1927, Ernst Schrödinger brilliantly adapted Maxwell's field equations to account for quantum field characteristics. At about the same time, Werner Heisenberg formulated matrix mechanics as another mathematical model of quantum wave behavior. In 1930, Paul Dirac integrated those models into a relativistic model of vector spaces, and the foundations of quantum mechanics were established.[10]

Quantum mechanics effectively describes the locality and non-locality of photons in a quantum field. Where a field is excited by a quantum of energy and momentum, it has finite degrees of freedom, implying that it is "there." As the photon escapes the boundaries of "there," it enjoys infinite degrees of freedom in a field that theoretically spans the entire universe! If it is detected in the back of my eye, it has finite degrees of freedom, so that its energy and momentum are "here."

The equations of quantum mechanics distill the mysteries of quantum reality into a mystery of quantum fields. Yet what is the essential nature

---

9. Hobson, "There Are No Particles," 213.
10. Hobson, "There Are No Particles," 215.

of the field so elegantly described by the equations? As Feynman said of Schrödinger's quantum wave equation, "Where did we get that equation from? Nowhere. It is not possible to derive it from anything you know. It came out of the mind of Schrödinger."[11]

Quantum Field Theory

> Today, all theories of elementary particles (such as the quark theory of matter) are quantum field theories. Particles are thought of as energetic excitations of the underlying field.[12]
>
> —John Polkinghorne

Quantum mechanics evolved into a broader theory describing interactions between fundamental particles, such as quarks, leptons, and bosons. According to quantum field theory, fundamental particles are essentially quantum fields, acting as particles only at points of interaction with other particle-fields. The implication is that reality at a most fundamental level consists of quantum fields.

Yet envisioning reality as fields raises ontological questions. Does a non-localized quantum field with infinite degrees of freedom exist in the same way as a localized field or particle? Does a photon field exist before and after it is excited by interaction with energy and momentum, or is it created at the moment of interaction? Are fields real, or are they merely mathematical constructs? Do fields generate physical reality only in interaction with other fields?

EMBRACING MYSTERY

> Reality, in fact, is usually something you could not have guessed. That is one of the reasons I believe Christianity. It is a religion you could not have guessed.[13]
>
> —C.S. Lewis

---

11. Wikipedia, "Schrödinger Equation."
12. Polkinghorne, *Quantum Theory: A Very Short Introduction*, 75.
13. Lewis, *Mere Christianity*, 32–33.

God inhabits mystery. God's essence is elusive, unknowable, incomprehensible. God's logic is impenetrable, sometimes defying our own. The depths of God are hidden, inaccessible except in observable interaction. Yet God gives life.

Now try something: In the previous paragraph, replace "God" with "light." Does the paragraph still make sense?

No one fully comprehends the nature of light, but everyone relates to light in practical ways. People plant flowers in sun or shade, assuming that light travels in a straight line from the sun. They eat plants without knowing or caring whether light acts like a wave or a particle. They put on polarized sunglasses or use lasers without realizing that they are taking advantage of the wave attributes of light. They don't worry about the mysteries of quantum field theory when they use transistors to amplify music, get an MRI at the hospital, or look at a picture on their phone.

Although God can be known in the simple faith of a child, his mysteries are inexhaustibly rich and powerful, for those who explore and embrace them.

Near

> People ... who, consciously or unconsciously, want to destroy
> Christianity ... put up a version of Christianity suitable for
> a child of six and make that the object of their attack.[1]
>
> —C.S. Lewis

WHEN I WAS EIGHT years old, I broke my arm while running home from school. A kind neighbor drove me to the hospital, and as the anesthesia began to take effect, I had a vivid dream of a rocket blasting into space. Just as the rocket was about to disappear from view, my perspective shifted; I caught up to the rocket, only to see it move even farther away. Over and over the cycle repeated; whenever it seemed I was getting closer to the rocket, it moved farther away.

I didn't think much about that drug-induced dream until five years later. By then I was thirteen years old, and I began to wonder where God was and how to reach him. I had learned at church that God was in heaven, and as my imagination traveled through space in search of heaven, it was always beyond my reach. My childhood dream became a paradigm for my quest; the closer I got to reaching God, the farther away he seemed.

Is God located somewhere in space—universe space? If his habitation is beyond the spatial boundaries of an immense universe, is he exceedingly far away? What kind of space does God inhabit?

---

1. Lewis, *Mere Christianity*, 32.

Near

Space beyond Space?

> But will God really dwell on earth with humans? The heavens, even the highest heavens, cannot contain you. How much less this temple I have built! Yet, Lord my God... Hear the cry and prayer that your servant is praying in your presence... Hear from heaven, your dwelling place.
>
> —King Solomon, 2 Chronicles 6:18–21

The temple represented God's presence among the people of Israel. In some sense, God was enthroned between the two gold cherubim above the Ark of the Covenant.

However, Solomon recognized that God could not be confined to the temple. God lived in heaven, beyond "even the highest heavens"—beyond the bounds of the universe. How then could he dwell in a temple in Jerusalem?

In his wisdom, Solomon did not allow his questions about God's dwelling space to derail his prayers. He believed that when God's people prayed at the temple, God heard their prayers in heaven. In reality, heaven was not so far away.

Yet the relationship between heaven and earth remains a mystery.

Comingled Spaces?

> Heaven... is God's space as opposed to our space, not God's location within our space-time universe. The question is then whether God's space and our space intersect; and if so how, when, and where... Heaven and earth are not coterminous, in this option. Nor are they separated by a great gulf. Instead, they overlap and interlock in a number of ways.[2]
>
> —N.T. Wright

Wright envisions heaven and earth as two separate spaces. Yet paradoxically, he says they "overlap and interlock." Since he cannot resolve the paradox, he acknowledges a mystery of "quasi-independent but mysteriously overlapping spheres."

---

2. Wright, *Simply Christian*, 59–63.

Wright raises the question of how God's space and our space intersect. Is God's space non-dimensional, an amorphous spiritual environment bleeding into the fabric of three-dimensional space? Are its dimensions beyond the weirdest science fiction, or are they in some way an extension of the space of the universe?

Definitive answers to those questions are beyond human comprehension, and certainly beyond the scope of this book. This chapter explores a model of multi-dimensional space, not to define God's space, but as a helpful model for imagining how God relates to people in the space they recognize.

HIGHER-DIMENSIONAL SPACE

> Branes are essentially membranes of lower-dimensional objects in a higher-dimensional space. (To picture this, think of a shower curtain, virtually a two-dimensional object in a three-dimensional space) . . . There are powerful reasons to believe there are extra dimensions in space.[3]
>
> —Lisa Randall

The holy grail of theoretical physics is to integrate two theories, general relativity and quantum mechanics, into a single "theory of everything." One approach is "string theory," which assumes a universe of at least ten dimensions, with the extra dimensions "curled up" so tightly within the universe that they cannot be detected. A more general approach, M-theory, assumes eleven dimensions.

Harvard physicist Lisa Randall theorizes that at least one of those extra dimensions might extend beyond the universe, and she uses that theory to explain the weak gravitational constant of quantum theory. She calls the higher-dimensional space the "bulk," and the observable space the "brane," short for membrane.

Higher-dimensional models provide a framework for representing relationships and interactions that are hidden in the observable universe. Higher dimensions are difficult to visualize, and physicists use abstract mathematical language to describe relationships. Yet a simple visual model of relationships between three-dimensional and two-dimensional spaces can be helpful in imagining relationships in higher dimensions.

---

3. Randall, "Theories of the Brane," 315–16.

Near

Flatland

In 1884, Edwin Abbott Abbott published a small book, *Flatland: A Romance of Many Dimensions*. The book was a social satire of Victorian culture, but its insights into the nature of multiple dimensions proved to be timeless.

Flatland is a two-dimensional world, with length and width, but no height. Flatland has points, which are tiny and appear the same from all directions. Line segments in Flatland have length, although their length appears shorter—even a point—as an observer moves around their endpoints. Triangles appear as line segments, but their lengths can never fully disappear. Circles appear as triangles, but their lengths do not change as an observer moves around them.

Viewing Flatland as a subspace of three-dimensional space, objects in Flatland also exist in 3-D space, with their true nature clearer from a 3-D perspective. An observer in 3-D can see that a triangle, which appears to a Flatlander as a single line segment of fluctuating length, is in fact three line segments, joined at their endpoints into a single object. An observer in 3-D can see that a circle is not at all like a line segment, but is actually a curved line. A Flatlander would never guess that unless he ran into it and found its curvature puzzling.

Higher Dimensions in Flatland

Flatlanders are not able to fully comprehend 3-D objects like spheres or cubes. Yet they might imagine, or even experience them, in these ways:

1. *Unseen proximity*: Objects might be a hair's breadth away in 3-D space, yet out of the view of Flatlanders. Flatlanders might be unaware of their existence—unless some mysterious "field" or shadow passed through Flatland.

2. *Intersections with 3-D Objects:* Three-dimensional solids might intersect Flatland in "slices." A sphere could intersect Flatland as a circle or point. Slices of 3-D objects would be very real in Flatland; yet Flatlanders would not be able to comprehend the depth of the solid object.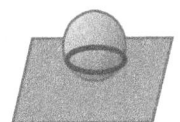

3. *Connected Movements*: A 3-D wire-frame cube might intersect Flatland in three points. The points would appear to Flatlanders as normal Flatland points, except that when the cube is moved, the points might all move, come together as one (but not two), or disappear! (Try it with your tissue box.) Movements that seemed to be connected in unexplainable ways might give hints of a reality in higher dimensions.

IMAGINING GOD IN HIGHER DIMENSIONS

> Now we see in a mirror dimly [literally, through a mirror in an enigma], but then face to face. Now I know in part; then I shall know fully, even as I have been fully known.
>
> —1 Corinthians 13:12 (ESV)

Imagine a Flatlander trying to comprehend a pet dog. Not only would the dog not fit into his world—it would not fit into his mind!

If a Flatlander happened to encounter a dog in some slice of reality, his encounter would be, at best, partial and enigmatic. His experience would fall far short of full comprehension, although it would be very real.

Michael Jastremski under CC BY-SA 3.0.

The God of the Bible is incomprehensible; he does not fit into human minds. Human concepts of God, no matter how vivid, do not capture the depth of his nature. For that reason, God commanded people not to make images of him, but to accept and know him as he reveals himself within the universe.

People encounter God in ways analogous to the ways a Flatlander might encounter objects in 3-D:

1. God in *unseen proximity*
2. God in the *intersections of life*
3. God in the *connected movements* of *human history*

1. God in *Unseen Proximity*

Imagine living within a "Flatland universe" of an oil painting. As you wander across the plane of the canvas, you move among colors and patterns, transitions, and mixtures of color. It is a beautiful and amazing universe, and only rarely do you imagine there might be anything beyond it.

Yet sometimes, as you wander across the canvas, the colors and patterns stir emotions and thoughts beyond logical explanations of "red next to green" or "color I haven't seen before." You sense there might be more to the design of the painting, and you cannot explain why. You sometimes observe the appearance of new colors or patterns, and they do not seem entirely random. Some fellow Flatlanders say they caught a glimpse of a painter or a paintbrush, which changed their view of the universe. And sometimes—is it your imagination?—it seems like an artist might be near enough that you can almost feel him breathing.

You begin to wonder: Might there be a reality beyond your 2-D "universe"? Would some of the patterns be clearer and lovelier from a perspective beyond the 2-D plane? Might there be an artist with a vision for the painting, fulfilling his vision with every stroke of the brush? Might he still be adding colors, shadings and details? Might he be near enough to breathe on the canvas?

An Unseen Artist?

> I wanted very much to learn to draw, for a reason that I kept to myself: I wanted to convey an emotion I have about the beauty of the world. It's difficult to describe because it's an emotion. It's analogous to the feeling one has in religion that has to do with a god that controls everything in the whole universe: there's a generality aspect that you feel when you think about how things that appear so different and behave so differently are all run "behind the scenes" by the same organization, the same physical laws. It's an appreciation of the mathematical beauty of nature, of how she works inside; a realization that the phenomena we see result from the complexity of the inner workings between atoms; a feeling of how dramatic and wonderful it is. It's a feeling of awe—of scientific

God through Cosmic Lenses

> awe—which I felt could be communicated through a drawing to someone who also had this emotion. It could remind him, for a moment, of this feeling about the glories of the universe.[4]
>
> —Richard P. Feynman

Although Feynman did not claim to believe in God, his feelings of awe and mystery resonate with those who sense God in unexplained wonder, transcendent beauty, and elegant wisdom.

Unexplained Wonder

> We are made of star-stuff.[5]
>
> —Carl Sagan

Why does stargazing move us? Why does the sound of ocean waves calm our spirits or a campfire engender peaceful reflection? Why does the wind blowing through the trees whisper to our hearts? What is there about a sunset or rainbow that causes us to take a picture and share it with friends?

In today's scientific age, we know a mountain is merely a bump on a planet, and the constellations of the ancients are actually stars unrelated to each other in space. Yet there is something about the sound of the wind and waves or the twinkling of stars in a very dark sky that touches a chord within us. Does God cause that chord to vibrate?

Transcendent Beauty

> I think that I shall never see a poem lovely as a tree.[6]
>
> —Joyce Kilmer

Instinctively, we recognize beauty in the physical world. We enjoy colorful flowers and beautiful sunsets, and we are fascinated by spider webs and dewdrops on leaves. When we see beautiful men or women, we can hardly

---

4. Feynman and Leighton, *Surely You're Joking*, 261.
5. Sagan, *Cosmic Connection*, 189.
6 Kilmer, "Trees," 160.

look away. We are captivated by magnificent architecture, graceful sculpture, and impressive laser light shows.

The beauty of the world extends far beyond human experience. Unique and colorful creatures inhabit the depths of the oceans, where no humans live to enjoy them—and they are more colorful and diverse than they need to be for survival. Galaxies and nebulae display beauty in spectrums of light only visible by humans when translated into visible colors.

Is the beauty of the universe the artistry of God?

Elegant Wisdom

> It seems to be one of the fundamental features of nature that fundamental physical laws are described in terms of a mathematical theory of great beauty and power... One could perhaps describe the situation by saying that God is a mathematician of a very high order, and He used very advanced mathematics in constructing the universe.[7]
>
> —PAUL DIRAC

Dirac was one of the pioneers of quantum physics, and a strident atheist. John Polkinghorne says of his teacher, "Dirac... once said that it was more important to have mathematical beauty in one's equations than to have them fit experiment!... Dirac made his many great discoveries, including the existence of antimatter, by a lifelong and highly successful quest for mathematical beauty."[8]

What makes an equation beautiful? Obviously, simplicity and utility—but what else? Does an equation that satisfies a yearning and stirs the imagination reflect the wisdom of an unseen God?

2. God in the *Intersections of Life*

In my office, I display a picture of my wife and myself on a sand dune on the Oregon Coast. People are drawn to it because it shows a loving couple at ease with each other. What they see is quite accurate—but it is only a

---

7. Dirac, "Evolution of the Physicist's Picture of Nature."
8. Polkinghorne, *Science and the Trinity*, 63–64.

small slice of a marriage relationship of over forty years. They don't see our younger years, our children, the challenges we faced together, or thousands of conversations and experiences we shared. They don't see our daughter, who took the picture, or the rest of our family and friends. They don't see all that was going through our minds at that moment—or at every moment of our lives. In fact, what they are seeing is not even our physical bodies, but a reflection of light from our bodies, passed through a lens onto a silicone memory chip, and then translated into a pattern of ink on a canvas. When they look at the picture, they are not seeing the totality of our lives, but our lives intersecting with a moment in time on an Oregon beach.

Although humans are not able to grasp the fullness of God, they can catch glimpses of him at particular times and places.

God in Mystical Experience

> Year of grace 1654 ... from about half past ten at night to about half an hour after midnight ... FIRE ... God of Abraham, the God of Isaac, the God of Jacob, and not of the philosophers and savants. Certitude. Certitude. Feeling. Joy. Peace ... God of Jesus Christ.[9]
>
> —Blaise Pascal

Pascal was a brilliant scientist, credited with groundbreaking work in probability, projective geometry, hydrostatics, and the philosophy of science. He did it all before his death at age thirty-nine!

Although Pascal's work was thoroughly grounded in the logic of mathematics and scientific methods, his experience taught him that God could not be limited by human reason. He famously said, "Reason's last step is the recognition that there are an infinite number of things which are beyond it ... The heart has its reasons, which reason does not know at all."[10]

---

9 Galli and Olsen, "Blaise Pascal," *131 Christians*, 114.

10. Galli and Olsen, "Blaise Pascal," *131 Christians*, 60–62.

Near

God in Inspiration

> I did think I did see all Heaven before me,
> and the great God himself.[11]
>
> —GEORGE FREDERICK HANDEL

By 1741, Handel was near bankruptcy, in great physical pain, and a victim of plots to sabotage his career. Deeply depressed, he was visited by his friend Charles Jennens. Jennens had written a libretto about the life of Christ and the work of redemption, with the text taken from the Bible. At the urging of Jennens, Handel agreed to compose music to match the text.[12]

A group of charities approached Handel to produce an upcoming benefit performance. Handel worked feverishly, and in twenty-four days he wrote two hundred and sixty pages of music. When he finished the Hallelujah Chorus, his assistant heard him say that he had seen God.

God Revealed Through Others

> Consciously, I am certainly an atheist, but I do not say it out loud, because if I look at Bach, I cannot be an atheist. Then I have to accept the way he believed. His music never stops praying. And how can I get closer if I look at him from the outside? I do not believe in the Gospels in a literal fashion, but a Bach fugue has the Crucifixion in it—as the nails are being driven in. In music, I am always looking for the hammering of the nails . . . That is a dual vision. My brain rejects it all. But my brain isn't worth much.[13]
>
> —HUNGARIAN COMPOSER GYÖRGY KURTÁG, 2015 INTERVIEW

Although Kurtág could not see God in Jesus or the gospels, he could sense the reality of God in Bach's music. Bach's experience with God was the lens through which Kurtág saw the love of God in the cross.

Many people open their minds to God because they see him through the life of someone else—a godly parent or grandparent, a teacher, a friend,

---

11 Galli and Olsen, *131 Christians*, 131.

12. Galli and Olsen, *131 Christians*, 131.

13. Meynell, *Wilderness of Mirrors*, 191.

or someone they find attractive. Others see God in a Christian group whose love and passion for goodness displays the character of God.

3. God in the *Connected Movements* of History

While I was writing, I heard a story of a young man in Haiti named Ronaldo. He was a shy young man, who somehow sensed that God wanted him to start a recycling company when he completed his schooling. He didn't know of any recycling companies in Haiti, and he didn't have any idea how to begin such a daunting project. Yet he reluctantly shared his dream with a Christian woman who gained his confidence.

That very week, an American businessman named Bill was visiting Haiti on a short term mission trip. Bill owned a recycling company in the United States! After meeting Ronaldo, he returned home and contacted the only recycling company in Haiti. Bill agreed to do some free consulting work for them if they would hire Ronaldo as an intern.

The events of the story seem quite disconnected at first. Bill goes into the recycling business, succeeds to the point of being interviewed by a trade journal, and decides to travel to Haiti after a hurricane. Ronaldo gives his life to Jesus, dreams of making a difference in the world, and reluctantly shares his dream with a woman, who connects him to a man that can help him turn his impossible dream into reality.

Coincidence—yes! Yet we can scarcely help but wonder whether every encounter and movement was part of God's unseen plan to help Ronaldo, give work to unemployed Haitians, and impact the environment.

Coincidence: Random Correlation or Connected Movements?

Many people say things like, "If this had been different..." or "It just seemed to work out." They might attribute remarkable coincidences to chance, or to a natural tendency to see patterns in the events of life. It is difficult to *prove* that God is behind events that coincide. Yet coincidences might indicate a higher plan and purpose intersecting human life, much like a cube intersecting and moving through Flatland.

Biblical Coincidence: Moses

> Moses said to God, "Who am I, that I should go to
> Pharaoh and bring the Israelites out of Egypt?"
>
> —EXODUS 3:11

Moses led the Israelites out of Egypt, and he was the author of portions of the first five books of the Old Testament. His story began at birth, when the daughter of an Egyptian Pharaoh saved him from death. His mother cared for him until he was weaned, and then he was raised in the royal court. As the adopted son of Pharaoh's daughter, he learned the culture and written hieroglyphic language of the Egyptians, as well as the art of war. When he took the side of his own oppressed people, he was forced to flee to the Sinai Peninsula, where he worked as a shepherd and learned to survive in the arid wilderness.

When God finally called Moses to lead his people out of Egypt, Moses was uniquely qualified for the job. He was able to speak confidently in the language of Pharaoh, guide the Israelites through an arid wilderness, wage war against enemies, and write a key portion of the Bible in the Hebrew language he helped shape. Those movements were part of God's plan to redeem his people from slavery in Egypt and make them into a nation for his glory.

Biblical Coincidence: Esther

> If you remain silent at this time, relief and deliverance for
> the Jews will arise from another place, but you and your
> father's family will perish. And who knows but that you
> have come to royal position for such a time as this?
>
> —ESTHER 4:14

God's people had sinned against God, and they were captives in the land of the Medes and Persians. The Persian king was displeased with his queen, and he held a beauty contest to replace her. Esther, a young Jewish woman, won the contest and was crowned queen of the Persian Empire!

The plot thickened: One of the king's advisors convinced the king to kill all the Jews in the kingdom. Esther's Jewish cousin heard of the plot and convinced her to ask the king to save her people. The Jews were saved by the king's decree.

Esther was an unlikely biblical hero: a beauty queen and concubine in the king's harem. She was reluctant to act until her uncle reminded her that there was more to life than her own safety. Yet as her uncle pointed out, the coincidence of her presence in the royal court at just the right time was an indication of a greater purpose.

The Book of Esther makes no mention of God. Yet it is not hard to see that the events in the story were connected by God's plan to save his people.

God's Grand Coincidence: Jesus Christ

> When the time had fully come, God sent his Son . . .
>
> —GALATIANS 4:4

When Jesus Christ was born, multiple strands of biblical history came together. Two thousand years before Jesus, God called Abraham and made a covenant promise to bless all the peoples of the world through him. Fifteen hundred years before Jesus sacrificed his life to redeem from sin, God told Moses to sacrifice a Passover lamb to redeem his people. One thousand years before Jesus arrived to initiate the kingdom of God, God promised David that one of his descendants would reign forever as king. About five hundred years before Jesus, Isaiah described in vivid detail a suffering servant, who would take upon himself the sin of the world. By the time Jesus was born, God's people were anxiously awaiting a Messiah, who would fulfill the Old Testament promises.

In secular history, the stage was set for the Christian movement. Greek was a universal language of trade over a broad area of the world, making possible wide distribution of the New Testament. The Roman Empire had developed roads and transportation systems, allowing the church to spread quickly. The Jerusalem temple and the Jewish establishment were destroyed a generation later, so Jews were no longer able to sacrifice animals or put their hope in an earthly kingdom. The Christian message of unselfish love, even for enemies, caused Christians to stand out in the following centuries, as plagues and wars struck the once-mighty Roman Empire.

Events that appeared to be unrelated were all part of God's glorious plan to save the world.

IS GOD REALLY THERE?

I began this chapter with a personal story of seeking a God I could not comprehend.

Although I thought God was far away, I was mistaken. I had two godly, unselfish parents, who reflected a love that went far beyond innate parental instincts. I had an active conscience, which troubled me at times and protected me often. I had a seeking mind, programmed to set out on a quest for spiritual truth, and I had a heart searching for a God I could not see. Perhaps most importantly, God gave me a healthy dissatisfaction with the over-simplified religious answers of my early childhood.

The story continued into my sixteenth year, when I finally decided to take a leap of faith and give my life to God. I was not at all sure God was real, and I was even less sure that what I had been taught about God could possibly be true.

That summer, I got my first job. There were fifteen of us, all about the same age. Through no merit of my own, I got a plum job: While others were scraping and painting bleachers until boredom set in, I was privileged to pick up garbage and unload it at the city dump with a pitchfork, riding around the rest of the day in an old Ford truck. I grew as a person that summer, as I found myself in a new and strange environment, and I learned to rely on God for guidance. I went on a youth retreat, where I experienced the warmth of Christian love and saw my sister and her fiancé exhibit Christian life as our leaders. I had an experience of beauty in the back seat of a Volkswagon bug on the drive home, when I saw, like never before, towering cumulus clouds against a deep blue sky.

With eyes of faith, I could finally see God's movement in my life.

Always

Your neighbors just got back from vacation, and they invited you to come over and look at their pictures—several hundred pictures. Honestly, you could find better pictures on the internet. You do not care about their pictures, because you did not share their experiences.

The couple they traveled with, however, will be very interested in the vacation pictures. Every picture brings back a memory of places they went and time they shared together.

Does God share time with people, or does he only look at snapshots of their activities? Does it even make sense to think that God can share time with people?

GOD AND TIME

> Remember the former things, those of long ago. I am God, and there is no other; I am God, and there is none like me. I make known the end from the beginning, from ancient times, what is still to come. I say: My purpose will stand, and I will do all that I please.
>
> —Isaiah 46:9–10

Isaiah's statement raises questions about how God interacts with the time of the universe. If he can see the entire history of the universe, is he beyond time? To accomplish his purposes, does he enter into the time sequence of the universe? Is God's time like ours, or entirely different?

Always

The Time Arrow of the Universe

Time is linear and sequential: Yesterday is followed by today and then tomorrow. Time is not static: Human history moves along a timeline from the past, through the present, and into the future.

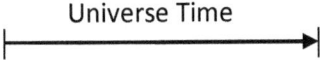

Humans are bound by the timeline of the universe. We can only *be present* in *the present*. We can neither see the future nor relive the past.

God in Extended Universe Time?

> Before the mountains were born or you brought forth the earth
> and the world, from everlasting to everlasting you are God.
> —Psalm 90:2

The writer of the psalm describes God's time as eternal, without beginning or end. He may have imagined God's time as an infinite extension of the human timeline.

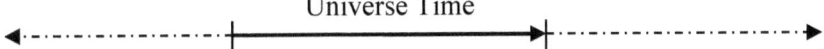

If God were bound to the timeline of the universe, however, he could not see or know what would happen in the future, and he could not effect change in the past.

God in Timeless Eternity?

> There is no time before the world ... Time does not
> exist without some movement and change ... God
> created the world with time rather than in time.[1]
> —Augustine of Hippo, Fourth Century

---

1. Augustine, *City of God*, XI.5, 6.

God through Cosmic Lenses

What was God doing ten minutes before he created the universe? When Augustine faced a similar question, he responded that the question was meaningless, because time began when the universe was created.

Time in the universe is marked by physical movement and change. Heavenly bodies are constantly in motion, and for millennia, people have tracked time by natural indicators like the rotation of the earth on its axis and the orbit of the earth around the sun. In the modern era, time in a quartz watch is referenced to the vibration of a crystal, 32,768 times per second.

Yet movement and change are not confined to the universe.

God Creates Time

> God does not live in a Time-Series at all . . . For his life is Himself.[2]
>
> —C.S. Lewis

God is not bound by time as an external constraint upon his being or action. Yet he is not bound by timelessness either, for that also would constrain him. He does not live in either time or timelessness; his life is himself.

Yet if movement and change define time, God creates time when he speaks or acts, whether in the universe or outside of it. The creation of the universe, for example, created a change in God's reality. One state of reality did not include a universe, and the other did. Neither state is "before" the other on the timeline of the universe, but the two states are distinct, not simultaneous, in God's time.

DEEPER TIME PERSPECTIVES

Chukovskaya via pixabay.com

---

2. Lewis, *Mere Christianity*, 131–32.

A jeweler assembling a bracelet creates a time sequence. The stone on the left begins the sequence, and each stone is added in own time, until the bracelet is completed.

A geologist can observe the time sequence of the jeweler, but he sees other time sequences as well. Each natural stone has its own history, formed over millennia through volcanoes, plant growth, floods, or glaciers. The second stone from the left might be the oldest, and the fourth stone might have taken longer to form than the first, even though they were discovered at the same time.

Looking at the bracelet, the geologist shares the time perspective of the jeweler, but he has a deeper time perspective on the stones, which the jeweler might not comprehend.

The analogy fits God, of course, for God's perspective on time is infinitely deeper than human comprehension. Unlike the geologist, God's perspective extends beyond the timeline of the universe.

Dimensions of Time

> It appears therefore more natural to think of physical reality
> as a four dimensional existence, instead of, as hitherto,
> the evolution of a three dimensional existence.[3]
>
> —ALBERT EINSTEIN

Einstein's theory of relativity linked three-dimensional space with one-dimensional time. The relationship between the dimensions of space and time is more complex than simple geometric models might suggest, but Einstein's theory supports Augustine's assertion that God created the universe "with time."

The time component of the universe is one-dimensional—an arrow of time. Although string theories imagine ten or eleven dimensions in the universe, no evidence has been discovered for any additional time dimensions in the universe. Beyond the space-time bounds of the universe, however, the possibility of multi-dimensional time cannot be excluded on scientific or philosophical grounds. The concept is intriguing, if only as a model for imagining time beyond the bounds of the space-time universe.

---

3. Lawson, *Relativity*, 171.

Time within Time

> If you picture time as a straight line along which we have to travel, then you must picture God as the whole page on which the line is drawn... God, from above or outside or all round, contains the whole line, and sees it all.[4]
>
> —C.S. Lewis

Lewis's analogy of time as a line drawn on God himself is awkward if pressed too far, but it suggests a simple model for the relationship between time in the universe and time outside the universe. In this model, universe time is a line drawn on the page of God's time. The line segment represents sequential, finite time, and the unbounded circle represents God's infinite, eternal time. The circle is two-dimensional, but higher or even infinite dimensions of God's time are possible.

Since God's time encompasses universe time, events on the timeline of the universe also occur in God's time, but events in God's time are not limited to the timeline of the universe. The geometry of the model is simple but thought provoking.

Imagining Multi-Dimensional Time

In the previous chapter, *Flatland* pictured ways in which inhabitants of a 2-D space might sense or experience 3-D reality. Near the end of the book, Edwin Abbott introduced *Lineland,* a 1-dimensional environment.

Lineland is less complicated, and we can imagine intersections of two-dimensional objects with Lineland. A two-dimensional object, such as a triangle or a circle, might intersect Lineland in two points, one point, or not at all. A triangle might also overlap in a line segment.

If the timeline of the universe is represented as a line segment and events in God's time are represented as two-dimensional shapes, intriguing relationships appear.

---

4. Lewis, *Mere Christianity*, 132.

Always

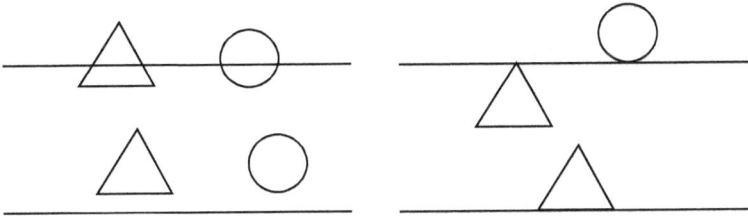

EVENTS IN GOD'S TIME

> With the Lord a day is like a thousand years,
> and a thousand years are like a day.
>
> —2 Peter 3:8

A picture pops up on social media. It features a couple in a fine restaurant, with the dashing young man on one knee and the ecstatic young lady slipping a ring onto her finger. They are engaged to be married, and the time stamp on the photo gives the date and time.

Yet for the young couple, the event is much more than the time stamp indicates. There was an awkward first date, a few disagreements, and long conversations. They shared joys and sorrows, expressed their love, and dreamed of a lifetime of commitment.

From the perspective of the camera, the couple's event was a single moment in time. Yet their perspective encompassed many more moments than the camera could convey.

Extending the analogy into God's time, events on the timeline of history have deeper significance in God's time. Abraham hears God speak. Moses sees a burning bush. Mary hears the first cry of baby Jesus. The meaning of those events extends beyond single moments in time, even into eternity.

A simple diagram illustrates an event from a dual perspective of God's time and universe time. An event in God's time might intersect the timeline of the universe as an event in human history, while the full significance of the event extends beyond universe time into God's multi-dimensional time.

The diagram seems superfluous, but it suggests another intriguing intersection. Just as a circle can intersect a line in two points, a single event in God's time might intersect the timeline of the universe at two separate points in universe time.

This kind of intersection gives insight into one of the most puzzling mysteries of the Bible.

The Intermediate State between Death and the Final Resurrection

> I desire to depart
> and be with Christ, which is better by far.
>
> —APOSTLE PAUL, PHILIPPIANS 1:23

My dad died a few years ago, at the age of ninety-four. Where is he now? Is he with Christ in heaven, or is he waiting for the second coming of Christ, the final judgment, and a perfected, spiritual body? The Bible gives answers that are difficult to reconcile with each other.

A thief, dying on a cross next to Jesus, asked Jesus to remember him when he came into his kingdom. Jesus replied, "Today you will be with me in paradise." When the apostle Paul faced the possibility of his death, he said, "I desire to depart and be with Christ, which is far better."[5] Both verses imply that believers are with Christ immediately after death.

Yet Paul also speaks of the future return of Christ, followed by the resurrection of believers: "I tell you a mystery: We will not all sleep, but we will all be changed—in a flash, in the twinkling of an eye, at the last trumpet. For the trumpet will sound, the dead will be raised imperishable, and we will be changed."[6]

If believers will be raised to life with new bodies at a time in the future of universe time, how can they already be alive with Christ immediately after their death? Paul must have recognized the apparent inconsistency—the paradox—of his own statements, but he was content to leave it as a mystery.

---

5. Luke 23:43, Phil 1:23.
6. 1 Cor 15:51–52.

Classical theologians tried to resolve the paradox by a theory of an *intermediate state* between death and the final resurrection. The theory utilized a non-biblical Greek concept of an immortal human soul, which could live apart from an earthly body. They speculated that the soul of a Christian goes to be with God in heaven at the time of death, where it remains until Christ returns to judge the living and the dead. Only after the judgment would the soul be joined to a resurrected body.[7]

That does not make sense to me! Is my dad less substantial now than when he inhabited a body on earth? If he is now in paradise, as Jesus promised, how would it be paradise if he were less than he was on earth?

In 2 Cor 5:2–4, Paul denies any interest in living as a soul without a body: "We groan, longing to be clothed with our heavenly dwelling, because when we are clothed, we will not be found naked. For while we are in this [bodily] tent, we groan and are burdened, because we do not wish to be unclothed but to be clothed with our heavenly dwelling, so that what is mortal may be swallowed up by life."

A theory of an intermediate state is inadequate because it supposes a bodiless existence between death and the final resurrection.

The Final Judgment as an Event in God's Time

> Christ died and returned to life so that he might be the Lord of both the dead and the living . . . We will all stand before God's judgment seat . . . each of us will give an account of ourselves to God.
>
> —Romans 14:9–12

I believe that, at this very moment in universe time, my dad is glorious in body and mind, enjoying paradise with Christ and the saints. If my dad is already with the Lord, it must be because, in some sense at least, the judgment of Jay E. Folkert has already taken place. On the other hand, biblical texts speak of a coming final judgment after Christ returns. From the perspective of universe time, the judgment of Jay appears as a paradox: He was judged when he died and went to be with the Lord, and he will be judged

---

7. *Heidelberg Catechism*, Q. 57. There is, however, some ambiguity in the catechism about when the soul is reunited with the body.

when Christ returns to judge everyone. Attempts to resolve the paradox have met with limited success.[8]

In God's time, however, the event of judgment can be pictured as a small circle intersecting the timeline of the universe at two points: the time of Jay's death, and the end of universe time, when Christ returns. When does my dad hear, "Well done, good and faithful servant"?[9] In the *event* of his final judgment. When does my dad receive his resurrected, perfected, spiritual body? In the *event* of his final judgment. When does my dad enter paradise? In the *event* of his final judgment. From a human perspective, judgment at his death is separated from judgment at the end of universe time. In God's time, judgment is a single event.[10]

How all of that works is a mystery to us. For Jay, it is no longer a mystery, but a joyful reality!

GOD AND HUMAN HISTORY

There are two ways to experience a basketball game.

A man at the game might be involved as a player, a coach, or a fan. He can participate in the game, sharing in the drama and excitement as the game develops. Even if all he does is cheer for his favorite team, he might influence the outcome. Of course, he doesn't know how the game will progress until the end of the fourth quarter.

The other way to experience the game is to watch a video replay. A man who watches the replay is not bound by the time progression of the game. He can know the scoring statistics and the final score, and even

---

8. Grudem, *Systematic Theology*, 1140–46. Grudem refers to Louis Sperry Chafer's dispensational view of three separate judgments, and Louis Berkhof's classical Reformed view of the final judgment as a formal, forensic display of God's justice.

9. Matt 5:21.

10. Polkinghorne says in *Exploring Reality*, 172: "Our time and the 'time' of the universe are, in general, associated with different dimensions of overall reality. It is conceivable, therefore, that though we all die at different times in this world, we shall all be re-embodied together at the same 'time' in the world to come. That would indeed be the Great Day of final resurrection."

watch some highlights, before he begins watching the game. He can skip the timeouts, freeze the action, and review key plays in slow motion. He can root for his favorite team and experience *some* of the drama and excitement of the game, but he is not a *participant* in the actual game, and he cannot influence the outcome in any way.

How is God involved in the game of life—the process of history? Does he participate in the drama of history as it unfolds, not knowing exactly how it will develop, or does he merely watch with interest from outside the timeline of the universe?

God above History

Classical theologians emphasized that God is not bound to the timeline of history. Boethius, an influential sixth century scholar and mathematician, wrote that God sees the progression of time *totum simul*—everything at once.

Theologian Wayne Grudem pictures God standing above time, with all of history equally present in his consciousness. He is careful to note, "God sees events *in time* and acts *in time*," but he adds, "He does not experience a succession of moments."[11]

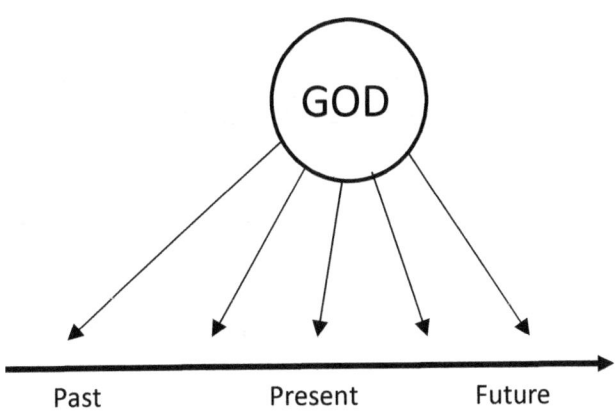

Grudem suggests an analogy of reading a long novel. After finishing the book, the reader can flip back through the pages, recalling events that transpired earlier in the book and making them all "present" in his mind. Yes, but the perspective of the reader is not the same. When we first

11. Grudem, *Systematic Theology*, 169–72.

encounter an event in a book, we are open to how the event might fit into the developing story. When we recall an event later, it is anchored in a completed storyline.

A God above history might see and act in history, but he would not experience history as it unfolds.

God in History

In the story of the Bible, God engages with history. Ungodly people do evil things, and God responds. God's chosen people sin, and God punishes and corrects. People pray, and God answers.

God is so deeply engaged in history that actions of people sometimes cause him to change his mind. While Moses was up on the mountain with God, the people persuaded Aaron to forge a golden calf that they worshipped. In response, God told Moses he would kill them all and replace them with Moses' descendants. Yet God's decision was not set in stone, for when Moses advocated for the people, "Then the LORD relented and did not bring on his people the disaster he had threatened." (Exod 32:14)

Although God has an unchangeable plan and purpose for human history, his plans are open to twists and turns along the way. He interacts with the procession of events in history to achieve his purposes.

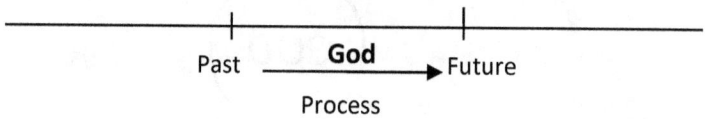

This picture of God in history has value, but it confines God to the timeline of the universe. From that perspective, he cannot see the whole picture, and he might be caught off guard by unexpected events. The picture also excludes God's actions outside of history.

God Both above and in History

To reconcile pictures of God above history and God engaged in history, some philosophers and theologians utilize a dipolar model of God's engagement with the timeline of the universe.[12] God's atemporal pole represents

12. Viney, "Process Theism."

his unchanging character and attributes, while his temporal pole represents his engagement in the history of the universe.

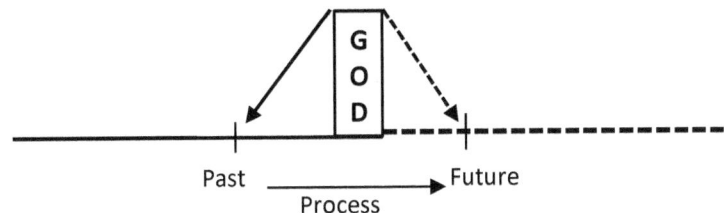

A dipolar concept of God combines the models of God above history and God in history, as it depicts both perspectives. Yet the model is not as neat as it seems. God's atemporal perspective would allow him to see the entire timeline of history in "an eternal Now,"[13] but from his temporal perspective, the future has not yet taken shape. To avoid the schizophrenia of God knowing, yet not knowing, the future, it seems that God can know only the past and the present, with perhaps a vague sense of the future.

A dipolar model illustrates profound truth about God, described by John Polkinghorne as, "mutual complementarity between the unchangingly steadfast and the providentially responsive."[14] Yet, while Polkinghorne affirms, "God will not be caught out by the movements of history into the future," the model limits God's awareness of a future not yet formed on the timeline of history.

God and History in the Perspective of Multi-Dimensional Time

The models we have considered so far view God's involvement in history solely from the perspective of universe time. The models create a false dichotomy: Either God interacts with history from within the limited perspective of a one-dimensional timeline, or he sees and engages with history from a timeless perspective.

The dichotomy stems from the limitations of human perspective. A simplified analogy is a grandfather, who invests in a college savings account at the birth of his infant granddaughter. The account existed primarily in the timeframe of the grandfather, impinging on the child's history when she learns of her grandfather's endowment, considers her college options, and

13. Lewis, *Miracles*, Appendix B.
14. Polkinghorne, *Science and the Trinity*, 105.

receives a receipt for tuition paid. From her perspective, the college account existed independently of her relationship with her grandfather, who held her as a baby, read her stories as a child, and encouraged her as a teenager. From the grandfather's perspective, however, the growing relationship and the growing balance in the account both express his love for her.

A model of multi-dimensional time views God's involvement in history from the perspective of God's time intersecting universe time. The model illustrates God's responsive participation in the process of history, as well as his steadfast plan and purpose "behind the scenes," which impinge upon it.

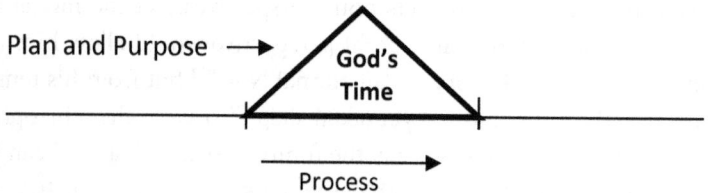

The biblical story of the Israelite journey from Egypt to the Promised Land illustrates these dimensions of God's interaction with history.

God participated in the process—the developing history—of the Exodus. He called Moses from the burning bush, sent ten plagues in response to the obstinacy of Pharaoh, and parted the sea to deliver the Israelites from slavery. He provided manna in an inhospitable wilderness, gave water when the people complained, and lengthened the wilderness wandering when they rebelled. The process of the Exodus was open to deviation, detours, and adaptations along the way.

Yet in another dimension of God's time, an unchanging promise guided his plan and purpose throughout the historical process. The promise emerged in human history when God said, "I have promised to bring you up out of your misery in Egypt into the land . . . a land flowing with milk and honey." (Exod 3:17) The promise endured in God's time, unaffected by the twists and turns of the wilderness. The enduring promise guided God's response in every situation, as he adapted his plan to achieve his purpose.

God's promise was unaffected by human history, but it intersected with history when Moses first repeated it, when God intervened in human affairs, and when the people finally crossed the Jordan and settled in the land God had promised them.

GOD AND PERSONAL HISTORY

The depth of God's time is somewhat like a father going for a walk with his young daughter. At every corner, they share life "in the moment," as they decide together which way to go next. Yet the father has other perspectives: experience, glimpses of the map on his phone, and knowledge of what time they left the house. In deeper perspective, he remembers the first time he held the child as an infant and a promise he made to his wife to bring the child home safely. He will guide the child as they make choices that will get them home in time for dinner. The girl can trust her father at every point in the journey.

As God walks with his children through life, his perspective is unbounded by human experience in time, and his interactions with his children are more profound. He sees their past and future, as well as pitfalls and possibilities along the way. He knows their state of mind—perhaps anxious, confused, energetic, bored, or rebellious. He has a plan and purpose, and he adjusts his plan to the choices they make.

This is a mystery beyond human comprehension, but if they trust him, he will get them home for dinner.

Infinite

> I have seen the burden God has laid on the human race.
> He has made everything beautiful in its time. He has
> also set eternity in the human heart; yet they cannot
> fathom what God has done from beginning to end.
>
> —Ecclesiastes 3:10–11

God is infinite. We are not.

This simple statement explains a great deal about why God is so hard to comprehend. Nothing in the universe is known to be infinite. The universe is huge by human standards—perhaps ninety-three billion light-years across—but not infinite. The scale of the smallest subatomic particles is incredibly small—but not infinitely small. The speed of light is amazingly fast—but not infinitely fast. The number of atoms in even a small diamond is so large that no one could count them in a lifetime—yet it is finite.

Since nothing in human experience is infinite, it is strange that humans have a concept of infinity. Does the concept of infinity point to something? Is there an infinite Reality beyond the universe? If there is, do the natural laws of the universe extend into that reality, or are they subsumed in deeper laws?

Infinity is weird.

> If any philosopher had been asked for a definition of infinity, he might have produced some unintelligible rigmarole, but he would certainly not have been able to give a definition that had any meaning.[1]
>
> —Bertrand Russell

For any finite number x,

$\infty + x = \infty$ and $\infty - x = \infty$

$\infty + \infty = \infty$

$\infty - \infty$ might equal ∞, or a finite quantity, or nothing at all

Obviously, infinity does not follow the rules of finite arithmetic. We should not expect that it would, since it is not a finite number and not actually a number at all. Infinity takes its meaning from what it describes. It is sort of like the concept of *depth*: We can speak of a *depth* of meaning, a *depth* of personality, or the *depth* of a submarine.

Although we might use poetry, art, or metaphor to imagine infinity, the most precise formulations of infinity use the language and images of mathematics. Whether in reference to counting numbers, geometric lines of infinite length, or limits approaching infinity in calculus, mathematics finds infinity to be a helpful concept.

SIMPLE MATHEMATICAL INFINITIES: NUMERICAL SETS

Numerical set theory provides an abstract framework for thinking about infinity. Even a child can understand counting, and counting is the foundation of a simple numerical set, the counting numbers: {1, 2, 3 . . .}.

The counting numbers are an infinite set. Based on the counting numbers, it is not hard to imagine a corresponding infinite set of negative numbers {-1,-2,-3 . . .}. Adding zero to the resulting union of the two sets yields the set of integers, visualized on a number line like this:

---

1. Mastin, "Bertrand Russell." Russell played a key role in the development of infinite mathematical set theory.

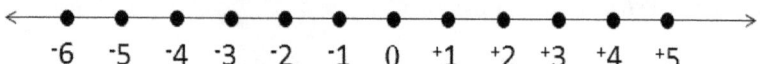

The set of integers is an infinite set, but it does not "fill" the number line. Based on the set of integers, another infinite set can be generated: the rational numbers. Each *rational* number is a *ratio* of two integers. For example, 2/3 is the ratio of 2 and 3, and 2.5 is the ratio of 25 and 10. The set of integers is a *subset* of the set of rational numbers, since each integer x can be described as the ratio x/1.

Rational numbers densely populate the number line. In fact, between any two rational numbers, there are an infinite number of rational numbers.

Although the rational numbers are very dense on the number line, other numbers that are not rational can be placed on the line. For example, π, which appears in nature as the ratio of the circumference of a circle to its diameter, has been proven not to be a ratio of any two integers. Its place on the number line is between 3.14159 and 3.14160.

The irrational numbers form an infinite set. The sets of rational and irrational numbers have no members in common, since logically a number cannot be both rational and irrational. However, the two sets overlap, and their members are infinitely "near" to each other. For any two rational numbers, there is an irrational number between them, and for any two irrational numbers, there is a rational number between them.

The union of the sets of rational and irrational numbers is a set called the *real numbers*. (Yes, there are imaginary numbers as well, but not on the same number line.) In a sense, the number line represents the "reality" of numbers.

Numerical sets demonstrate relationships between sets, even non-numerical sets.

1. *Subsets.* Since every member of the set of counting numbers also belongs to the set of real numbers, the set of counting numbers is a subset of the set of real numbers. The set of rational numbers and the set of irrational numbers are also subsets of the set of real numbers.

2. *Disjoint sets.* Although the sets of rational numbers and irrational numbers overlap on the number line, they have no members in common.

3. *Relationships between disjoint sets.* The set of rational numbers and the set of irrational numbers do not intersect. Yet since both are subsets

of the set of real numbers, the rules of arithmetic for the set of real numbers apply across the boundaries of the two subsets. For example, 2 is a rational number, $\sqrt{2}$ is an irrational number. $2\sqrt{2}$ is irrational, and surprisingly, $\sqrt{2} \cdot \sqrt{2} = 2$, a rational number.

GOD'S INFINITE REALITY

Although the infinity of God's reality is qualitatively different from the infinity of numerical sets, relationships between numerical sets suggest analogous relationships between the universe and God's reality:

1. The universe is a subset of a larger reality.
2. God is everywhere, but God and the universe are distinct from each other.
3. God connects earth and heaven.

1. The universe is a subset of reality.

> Who has measured the waters in the hollow of his hand,
> or with the breadth of his hand marked off the heavens?
> Who has held the dust of the earth in a basket, or weighed
> the mountains on the scales and the hills in a balance?
>
> —ISAIAH 40:12

The universe is incredibly large, but finite. Is the universe part of a larger reality? If so, what is the relationship of the universe to that reality, and how does human life fit into it?

Does the Universe = All of Reality?

> The universe is all there was, and is, and ever will be.
>
> —THE BERENSTAIN BEARS, QUOTING CARL SAGAN

God through Cosmic Lenses

> I have a friend, a good friend, who's an extremely good scientist who's an evangelical Christian. So we all understand one thing: that the whole point of science, the whole game that we're playing, is to try to explain nature without introducing what I call the "supernatural." It is what science is.[2]
>
> —Leonard Susskind

In the first microseconds of the finite universe, the entire reality of the universe was trillions of trillions of times smaller than the head of a pin. (Of course, pins did not exist at that time; nothing in the universe provided a larger frame of reference!) Was there anything else beyond that almost infinitesimal universe? The tools of science cannot answer that question, since they are effective only *within* the universe.

Reality beyond the universe is certainly possible, and some speculate that the universe arose naturally from quantum uncertainty in a larger environment, following the same laws of nature as the universe we inhabit.[3] That supposes, however, that the laws of quantum behavior existed in a preceding "universe," or that they exist in a larger environment.

It is not unreasonable to assume that our universe is a subset of a larger reality. Since science is limited to the bounds of the universe, reality is inherently unknowable, except as it intersects the universe. Reality might also be revealed "supernaturally" by revelation within human history.

If infinite reality exists, it provides a canvas for exploring questions about origins, meaning, human values, and eternal existence. If the universe is all there is, answers to those questions are elusive.

Is the Universe a Virtual Reality?

In virtual reality games, players choose a character or an avatar and construct a virtual life. They build houses, gain skills, and even develop complex personalities. Their world is filled with props: other characters, animals, weapons, money, and belongings. They make decisions about jobs and recreation, and they create new things. They live a virtual life—until the computer crashes and life evaporates into nothingness

---

2. St. Louis Chronicle, "Physicist Plucks Away at our Tightly Strung Universe."

3. Krauss, for example, proposes a universe arising from a quantum vacuum, assuming its existence outside the universe.

Infinite

If life on earth is a virtual reality, people, animals, and objects are like game pieces to be manipulated and used for maximum benefit. Anything of lasting value must be translated to true reality before the game ends. Religious people might hope to gain a "ticket to heaven" or invest wealth and success in eternal things. Nonreligious people will simply try to enjoy the game while it lasts.

Is the Universe a Subset of Reality?

If the universe is a subset of a larger reality, events in the universe take place simultaneously in a larger reality as well.

I know a family that adopted six children from other countries, all with special needs. One of the girls was adopted at the age of two, and she had never been outside the walls of an orphanage in Mongolia. She could not imagine anything beyond the orphanage, but while she was living there, she was also living in a broader world. Today, she has few conscious memories of the orphanage, but the impact of her experiences continues beyond the orphanage walls.

Life on the earth takes place within a larger reality.

Human Impact in Reality

> The heavens will disappear with a roar; the elements will be destroyed by fire, and the earth and everything in it will be laid bare. Since everything will be destroyed in this way, what kind of people ought you to be? You ought to live holy and godly lives as you look forward to the day of God and speed its coming. That day will bring about the destruction of the heavens by fire, and the elements will melt in the heat. But in keeping with his promise we are looking forward to a new heaven and a new earth, the home of righteousness.
>
> —2 Peter 3:10–13

Why do Christians care for the earth? If the universe ("the heavens") is going to be destroyed eventually, and Christians are looking forward to a new heaven and a new earth, isn't the earth disposable?

If the universe is a subset of reality, the earth has a transitory but real existence in both the universe and the larger reality. Everything that happens on the earth also happens in God's eternal reality.

Imagine a group of toddlers on a playground. The world is much bigger than the few thousand square feet within the fence. Yet today, as they play in their own little universe, they are also living in a reality beyond their playground, making a tiny but real impact upon the entire world. Personalities are being formed. Teachers, parents, and grandparents will be affected by their behavior. The collective culture of the entire world will experience a tiny ripple from the actions of the toddlers within their tiny universe. Even though the playground might be paved over for parking in a year or two, the world will be changed by what happens there today.

If the universe is a subset of reality, actions on earth have enduring impact in God's reality. Caring for a pet dog has eternal significance, even if dogs don't go to heaven. Using natural resources wisely, taking care of one's body, and feeding hungry people have an impact extending beyond the boundaries of the earth.

Christians care about the earth for reasons quite different from some other philosophies or religions. They do not worship the earth as a god or ultimate reality. They do not think of themselves as one with the earth. They do not believe the earth will endure forever. They see themselves as stewards of the earth, whose faithful care in the transitory universe has eternal, cosmic consequences.

2. God is everywhere, but God and the universe are distinct from each other.

> There is . . . one God and Father of all, who is
> over all and through all and in all.
>
> —EPHESIANS 4:5

How is God related to the universe? Is he distant and inaccessible, locked up in a far-off heaven, disconnected from everyday life? Or is he found in every blade of grass, every thought or feeling, every quantum field or spinning quark?

Infinite

The apostle Paul gives a paradoxical, almost mysterious answer: *God is over all and through all and in all*. Since he is *over* all, God is beyond the universe; yet in some way, God is *through* and *in* the universe.

In more technical language, God is both *transcendent* (above or beyond) and *immanent* (with or in). This is a paradox, of course, which some try to resolve by elevating one attribute at the expense of the other.

Transcendence over Immanence

> Our God is in heaven; he does whatever pleases him. But
> their idols are silver and gold, made by the hands of men.
>
> —Psalm 115:3–4

The Bible says God is in heaven, holy (literally, set apart), and not confined to buildings or manmade images. This causes some people to think God is far away, beyond the far-off boundaries of the universe. As a far-off God, he seems inaccessible, uninvolved in everyday life.

In practical terms, elevating God's transcendence over his immanence makes God quite irrelevant to everyday life. A personal relationship with him would be like a college student far from home, living on her own and texting her father only when she needs money.

Immanence over Transcendence

> I celebrate myself; and what I assume, you shall assume; for
> every atom belonging to me, as good belongs to you.[4]
>
> —Walt Whitman, Leaves of Grass

Some people identify God with nature, with wisdom, with forces in the universe, or with their own experiences. The idea is found in poets such as Whitman and Emerson, in religions such as Advaita Vedanta Hinduism and Sufi mysticism, and in movies such as *Star Wars* and *The Lion King*.[5]

Beliefs that emphasize the immanence of God fall into a wide range:

---

4 Whitman, *Leaves of Grass*, 25.
5. Mander, "Pantheism."

- Pantheism, from the Greek *pan* (all) and *theos* (god), which more or less equates God with all of reality, including the universe.
- Panentheism, from *pan* + *en* (in) + *theos*, which can be defined as the belief that "the Being of God includes and penetrates the whole universe, so that every part of it exists in Him, but His Being is more than, and not exhausted by, the universe."[6]
- The idea that God is in the process of himself being created, by the influence of the world upon him.
- Less-defined popular beliefs, expressed in statements like, "I think you can see God in everything," or "God is whatever you think he is."

In practical terms, elevating God's immanence over his transcendence makes God in the image of his creation, either the universe or humanity. God is identified with nature, emotions, awe and wonder, or fate. Prayer is like talking to oneself or the wind, and worship is like getting in touch with one's surroundings.

Does ∞ = All?

> It turns out to be impossible to conceive of God as fully infinite if he is limited by anything outside himself.[7]
>
> —Philip Clayton

Philip Clayton is an eminent *panentheist*. His imprecise description of God as "fully infinite" fails to recognize that infinite sets are not necessarily all-inclusive. For example, the set of rational numbers is unlimited, both in density (There is always another number between two elements.) and in extent (There is always a number that is greater than any element.). Yet it is limited, by definition, to exclude the set of irrational numbers.

God defines boundaries for himself, with the created order not part of his infinite Being. Thus nature is distinct from God—not because nature excludes him, but because God chooses not to share his identity with nature. If nature were part of God's being, God would have added to himself when he created the universe. Instead, God created a universe apart than himself.

---

6. Cross and Livingstone, *Oxford Dictionary of the Christian Church*, 1213.
7. Polkinghhorne, *Science and the Trinity*, 96.

Infinite

C.S. Lewis says it quite eloquently, referring more narrowly to pantheism:

> Pantheists usually believe that God, so to speak, animates the universe as you animate your body; that the universe almost *is* God, so that if it did not exist He would not exist either... The Christian idea [is that] God invented and made the universe—like a man making a picture or composing a tune. A painter is not a picture, and he does not die if his picture is destroyed. You may say, "He's put a lot of himself into it," but you only mean that all its beauty and interest has come out of his head. His skill is not the picture in the same way that it is in his head, or even in his hands.[8]

God is near, yet distinct from his creation.

> The God who made the world and everything in it is the Lord of heaven and earth... he is not served by human hands, as if he needed anything, because he himself gives all men life and breath and everything else... God did this so that men would seek him and perhaps reach out for him and find him, though he is not far from each one of us. "For in him we live and move and have our being."
>
> —ACTS 17:24–28

A man goes into a quiet room, to pray or meditate. What is the point of the exercise? Is he connecting with the God within him or the God of collective consciousness? Are his prayers disrupting the flow of the universe, gathering and releasing cosmic energy? Is he sending a long-distance message to heaven, hoping to convince a far-off God to show up in the universe and do something special?

The Bible indicates that God is near, yet separate from the universe. God is beyond the man's consciousness; yet his knowledge penetrates the man's deepest thoughts. God is not collective human consciousness, although others may be praying with the man. The man's prayers do not directly influence the forces of the universe or change the course of history, although his requests are woven into God's plan and purpose.

---

8. Lewis, *Mere Christianity*, 30.

Simply put, the man is not merely talking to himself, or the universe, or to a God who is uninvolved in the man's environment. He is talking to a God that is near, yet distinct from the man and his world.

3. God connects heaven and earth.

> The seventy-two returned with joy and said, "Lord, even the demons submit to us in your name." Jesus replied, "I saw Satan fall like lightning from heaven."
>
> —LUKE 10:17–18

Heaven and earth are separate realms; they do not intersect. Yet Jesus said that as the disciples overcame demons in the earthly realm, Satan suffered defeat in the heavenly realm.

Both heaven and earth exist in a larger reality, and God rules over both. Actions on earth have impact in heaven, and events in heaven alter history on earth.

The connection between events in heaven and earth is that both are ruled by God.

Heaven Touching Earth

> Jesus went into Galilee, proclaiming the good news of God. "The time has come," he said. "The kingdom of God has come near. Repent and believe the good news!"
>
> —MARK 1:14–15

Jesus spoke often about the *kingdom of God*. God's kingdom is not a place; it is life under the authority of God as King. In heaven, the dominion of God is fully realized; on earth, rebellion causes anarchy and evil.

Jesus brought the kingdom of God into the world, as he was fully obedient to his Father and exercised the authority of his King. The kingdom rule of God spanned heaven and earth.

Jesus demonstrated life in God's kingdom. Near the beginning of his ministry, he went into the synagogue at Capernaum with his disciples. Afterwards, he went to Peter's house. Peter's mother-in-law was in bed with a fever, and when they told Jesus, he went in, took her hand, and helped her up. The fever left her, and she was able to serve dinner. After sunset, people began to come to the door of the house—people who were sick or oppressed by evil. One by one, Jesus healed those who had various kinds of diseases, and drove out many demons. For Peter and the other disciples, it must have been like a slice of heaven!

When Jesus came to a town, sick people were healed, sinners were restored, outcasts were loved, and confused souls found truth that set them free. All heaven broke out—because wherever Jesus was, heaven broke into the world.

Earth Reaching for Heaven

> Your kingdom come, your will be done on earth as it is in heaven.
>
> —MATTHEW 6:10

The kingdom reign of God is not fully realized on earth. Human rebellion resists God's authority, allowing anarchy and evil to reign. Jesus told his disciples to pray for the will of God to be done, so that the blessings of heaven would extend to life on earth.

Earth becomes more like heaven when people trust and obey the King. The church of Jesus Christ should be an environment where people get a taste of life in the kingdom of God. Then someday, when the King comes in his glory, they will enter into the fullness of the kingdom.

LIVING THE MYSTERY OF EARTH AND HEAVEN

> The kingdom of God is . . . righteousness,
> peace and joy in the Holy Spirit.
>
> —ROMANS 14:17

I experienced a slice of heaven in a laundromat.

When I was single, our group of Christian young adults went on a camping trip to the upper peninsula of Michigan. We took a ferry to Mackinac Island, where we planned to spend the day exploring. Mackinac Island has no cars, only horses and bicycles, so we rented tandem bicycles and took off through the streets and hills. Soon it started to rain, and we discovered that horses leave a residue on streets, which tends to splash up when it rains! We decided to leave the island, only to find that hundreds of other people had made the same decision. We were forced to wait a long time for a ferry, in the cold, damp, windy weather.

Our clothes were soaked and dirty, so we went together to a laundromat. Someone broke out some playing cards, and we began to play *Spit on Your Neighbor* (later commercialized as *Uno*). Despite the name of the game, something heavenly happened. We were warm and dry—and we were loved and safe. No one was alone, no one was better than anyone else, and no one was judged for how they looked or how successful they were. No one was trying to make a good impression or climb a social ladder.

The kingdom God is, as the apostle Paul said, "righteousness, peace, and joy in the Holy Spirit." The kingdom broke out in our group that day, and as time went on it spread into the world, as the people of that group went out in service to their heavenly King.

Personal

Woody Allen's movie Sleeper presents a scene in which Woody, cryogenically frozen, goes through old photos trying to explain his era to residents of the world two hundred years later. He comes across a photo of a famous evangelist, [and comments], "Billy Graham. Claimed to know God personally." Invariably the movie audience laughs.[1]

—Philip Yancey

Why does the audience laugh? They can't imagine a personal God, and they can't imagine that a mere human could know him personally.

When God appears personally in the movies, he is portrayed as an interesting human being. In *Bruce Almighty*, he is a genial, deep-voiced old man, played by Morgan Freeman. In *Oh, God*, he is a crotchety yet endearing George Burns. In *Almost an Angel*, he takes the traditional form of Charlton Heston, with flowing robes and curly gray hair. In *Skidoo*, he is a cigar-chomping, drug dealing Groucho Marx.

It is hard to imagine an old man like Morgan Freeman or George Burns as the source of a universe that inspires awe and wonder or the power that overcomes evil and makes all things right. God's person-ality does not imply that he is like our friends Bob or Sally, who have strange quirks and forget where they left their keys. God's person-ality is powerful: his words shake the mountains and his thoughts are precious.

1. Yancey, *Reaching for the Invisible God*, 31.

God through Cosmic Lenses

What does it mean, then, to say that God is personal? Person-ality is surprisingly hard to define. Negatively, a personal God is not merely an *impersonal* force, a cipher for the laws of nature, or a universal principle. Positively, a personal God has self-consciousness, a will, and the ability to act. Most importantly, a personal God can know and be known by other persons.

HOW CAN HUMANS KNOW GOD PERSONALLY?

Our family was visiting the Henry Ford Museum in Dearborn, Michigan. As we wandered through the display of *Mathematica*, I saw a familiar face and name on one of the displays. I grabbed my son and his wife, pointing at the picture and exclaiming, "I knew Norbert Wiener personally."

Norbert Wiener was a child prodigy and a professor of mathematics at MIT. He coined the word "cybernetics," an interdisciplinary formalization of feedback theories, with applications in such disparate fields as mechanical systems, behavioral psychology, data compression, and artificial intelligence. Dr. Wiener was also an important figure in the development of set theory and chaos theory, which are touched upon in this book.

I knew none of those things when I met Dr. Wiener in 1963, shortly before his death. Computers were beginning to make their way into colleges and universities, and my father drove our family two thousand miles to attend a National Science Foundation summer institute at UCLA. We had an apartment near the campus, and my parents gave their twelve-year-old son free rein within the open courtyard. One evening, I met an older gentleman, and we began to talk. He was personable, interested in knowing what I was thinking, and eager to talk about his life and work. I was fascinated when he told me he could lecture in seven languages and speak five fluently. I asked him whether it was easier to go from one language to another when they were similar, and he said the opposite was true; similar languages could be confusing.

We talked more than once, and after our first conversation, my father was surprised to hear that I had been talking with the legendary mathematician who was lecturing at the NSF institute. I did not know Dr. Wiener's thought processes as a mathematician or a scientist, as I could only comprehend arithmetic and basic science. Dr. Wiener connected with me on my level, and I knew him personally as a gentle, perhaps lonely old man, who found time to talk to a curious twelve-year-old boy.

Personal

For humans to know God personally, God must condescend to meet them in ways they can understand. He condescends to their knowledge and intellect, speaking in common language. He condescends to their understanding of the universe, describing his reality in images they can fathom. He condescends to their cultural worldview, revealing his character in the context of their social order.

Envisioning a Personal God in a Pre-Scientific Worldview

> In ancient times, the world must have seemed pretty arbitrary. Disasters such as floods or diseases must have seemed to happen without warning, or apparent reason. Primitive people attributed such natural phenomena to a pantheon of gods and goddesses, who behaved in a capricious and whimsical way.[2]
>
> —Stephen Hawking

Ancient people were aware of patterns in nature, such as the seasons and lunar months, the constellations and movement of the sun, and the impact of rain on crop production. Myths about gods explained the origins of the earth, the seasons, natural disasters, misfortune and good luck.

As products of human imagination, the gods acted much like humans. They were unpredictable, conflicted, needy, and grasping for power. They were sometimes moody or inattentive, effecting chaos and disorder in nature.

Nature religions employed rituals as a kind of technology. Through incantations, sacrifices, fertility rites, or rain dances, they invited their gods to bring babies, rain, good crops, or victory over their enemies.

God is unlike nature gods, but in the Old Testament he revealed himself to people within their prescientific worldview.

A Dependable God

> There was evening, and there was morning ... As long as the earth endures, seedtime and harvest, cold and heat, summer and winter, day and night will never cease.
>
> —Genesis 1 and 8:22

2. Hawking, "Does God Play Dice?"

The biblical account of creation is unlike other ancient accounts, which are unruly and tumultuous. Genesis 1 emphasizes that God brought order out of chaos. By his command, he separated light from darkness, established day and night, and marked off seasons, days, and years. He made flora and fauna to replicate "according to their kinds." He called the order and the structure of the universe "very good."

When Noah came out of the ark after a catastrophic flood, God assured him that the world would continue to operate according to what are known today as the laws of nature. The God of the Bible is dependable, not whimsical. He is able to do whatever he pleases, and he is pleased to establish and support the laws of nature.

A Powerful God

> When all the people saw this, they fell prostrate and cried, "The LORD—he is God! The LORD—he is God!"
>
> —1 KINGS 18:39

Drought had come to the land of Israel, and the people had sought relief from Baal, the god of fertility and rain. Finally, God's prophet Elijah challenged four hundred and fifty prophets of Baal to a faceoff, where each would prepare an offering of a bull and call upon their god to burn the offering with fire. All morning long, the prophets of Baal prayed, shouted, and danced around their altar, to no effect. Elijah goaded them, saying, "Shout louder! Surely he is a god! Perhaps he is deep in thought, busy, or traveling. Maybe he is sleeping and must be awakened." The desperate prophets shouted louder and cut themselves with swords and spears, to no avail.

Finally, at the time of the evening sacrifice, Elijah rebuilt the altar of Yahweh, using twelve stones to represent the twelve tribes God had chosen. He humbly prayed to the God of Israel, asking him to send fire to burn the offering. God did it! The Israelites fell down in awe and rose up to slaughter the prophets of Baal. Then, to top it all off, Elijah bowed in prayer, asking God seven times to break the drought and bring rain. God did that too, as a final kick in the teeth to the fertility god Baal, whose specialty was supposed to be rain.

Would God do something like that today? Why would he? The worldview of most people is not structured around gods of nature, but laws of nature. God interacts with people within their cultural worldview, revealing himself in ways they can understand.

A Faithful God

> Lord, the God of Israel, there is no God like you in heaven above
> or on earth below—you who keep your covenant of love with
> your servants who continue wholeheartedly in your way.
> —King Solomon, 1 Kings 8:23

When Solomon compared the God of Israel with the gods of other peoples, there was really no comparison. Other gods were self-serving and capricious, but Israel's God was faithful and trustworthy.

God's covenant of love was a personal commitment made to Abraham two thousand years before Christ. God's personal commitment was the foundation of the exodus from Egypt, the royal line of King David, and eventual fulfillment in Jesus Christ. His commitment never wavered with the passage of time.

In a pre-scientific worldview, the existence of a personal God was not difficult to imagine. The uniqueness of the God of the Bible was his faithful, dependable character and his power to act in history.

Envisioning a Personal God in the Worldview of Classical Science

> Nature can only be commanded by obeying her.
> —Sir Francis Bacon, Novum Organum, 1620

Classical science is based on the conviction that nature is not random or capricious; events occur according to unchanging laws of nature.

Scientific thought was not unknown to ancient people. Names like Archimedes, Ptolemy, Hippocrates, Galen, Aristotle, Pythagoras, and Euclid are still remembered in the western world. Scientists in the Arab world are less well known, but astronomy, Arabic numerals, and the concept of zero developed in the East.

Science took a great leap forward in the Scientific Revolution, beginning in the late sixteenth century. Advances in technology led to new discoveries, and wider dissemination of knowledge allowed observations and theories to be published and critically discussed. An empirical scientific method gained wide acceptance, with theories confirmed by repeated experiments.

The Scientific Revolution generated laws or principles to describe the structure and operation of nature. Laws of nature are valid throughout the universe and apply invariably in wide-ranging circumstances.

I have a pool table in my basement. Although I cannot claim to be a good player, I am good at figuring the angles. When the ball doesn't go where I intended, I don't blame it on the pool gods. I believe the laws of nature operate in my basement, so if the ball doesn't end up in the pocket, I must have aimed wrong, the cue stick is crooked, or (my favorite excuse) the cheap table isn't perfectly flat.

The laws of nature apply, not only on pool tables, but throughout the universe. In 1687, Sir Isaac Newton published *Principia*, considered by many to be a "grand synthesis" of the Scientific Revolution. From his observations and the work of others, Newton identified three laws of motion. Newton's laws describe the behavior of pool balls, adjusting for things like friction and uneven tabletops. More remarkably, Newton's laws apply everywhere in the universe. Utilizing his laws of motion, his law of gravitational attraction, and some analytical geometry, it is possible to predict the movement of the planets around the sun!

Modern science is based upon a belief that laws of nature consistently predict or determine events. The laws apply throughout the universe; they don't depend upon whether it is Tuesday or a ghost is passing through. They are as dependable as the movement of the planets.

How is God envisioned in the worldview of classical science?

God as the Source of the Laws of Nature

> This most beautiful system of the sun, planets, and comets,
> could only proceed from the counsel and dominion of
> an intelligent Being... This Being governs all things,
> not as the soul of the world, but as Lord over all.
>
> —Sir Isaac Newton, Principia

Many scientists of the Scientific Revolution were Christians, and they recognized God as the Source and Sustainer of the laws of nature. All three founders of heliocentric cosmology—Copernicus, Kepler, and Newton—viewed the universe as an offshoot of their theology. Rene Descartes (1596–1650) explicitly related his law of inertia to the sustaining power of God.

From the time of Descartes onward, "The Watchmaker" was a common analogy for God as the Source of nature and its laws. As a watchmaker designs and manufactures a watch and winds it up, God skillfully designed and created the universe, including the laws by which it operates.

William Paley popularized the analogy of the watchmaker in his book, *Natural Theology*, published in 1802. He argued that the intricate design of living things is evidence of a Creator who cares for every creature: "The hinges in the wings of an earwig, and the joints of its antennae, are as highly wrought, as if the Creator had nothing else to finish. We see no signs of diminution of care by multiplicity of objects, or of distraction of thought by variety. We have no reason to fear, therefore, our being forgotten, or overlooked, or neglected."[3] Paley's book was a best seller for most of the nineteenth century, and it generated great interest in the natural sciences among Christians.

The watchmaker analogy identifies God as the Source of the universe and its laws. Does the watchmaker continue to be active in a developing universe, where life evolves?

God and Evolutionary Processes

> There is grandeur in this view of life, with its several powers, having been originally breathed by the Creator into a few forms or into one; and that, whilst this planet has gone cycling on according to the fixed law of gravity, from so simple a beginning endless forms most beautiful and most wonderful have been, and are being, evolved.[4]
>
> — CHARLES DARWIN, THE ORIGIN OF SPECIES, SECOND EDITION

Charles Darwin had been impressed by Paley's watchmaker argument, but he found in natural selection a more satisfying explanation for the diversity of life. Yet Darwin left room for a Creator—a Creator of a universe designed to generate beauty, variety, and increasing complexity.

Evolutionary concepts were not new. Christian theologians in the fourth century, such as Gregory of Nyssa and Augustine, saw evolution

---

3 "William Paley," University of California Museum of Paleontology.
4 Darwin, *Origin of Species*, 307.

in Genesis. Lamarck, a French naturalist, had proposed a later-disproven evolutionary theory earlier in the nineteenth century. Yet natural selection challenged religious and scientific assumptions about the origins of life.

Early Darwinian theories were simplistic, with evolution crudely depicted as fish growing legs and humans descending from apes. The intricacy and complexity of evolutionary processes were not yet known, leading to a loss of awe and wonder at the design of a universe capable of producing life.

Later discoveries revealed more complex and profound processes in evolutionary development. Dr. Francis Collins, Director of the Human Genome Project that mapped the three billion biochemical letters of human DNA, writes, "God . . . created the universe and established natural laws that govern it. Seeking to populate this otherwise sterile universe with living creatures, God chose the elegant mechanism of evolution to create microbes, plants, and animals of all sorts."[5]

Scientists like Collins integrate science and faith, but many people struggle to reconcile the two, elevating one over the other or relegating them to separate realms of knowledge.

Separate Domains?

The Origin of Species was published in 1859, when science was emerging from the shadows of philosophy and religion. Earlier in the Scientific Revolution, the church had controlled the universities, and those studying the natural sciences were known as "natural philosophers." Eighteenth-century philosophers Immanuel Kant and Jean-Jacques Rousseau had argued that science and religion were two separate domains, and in the nineteenth century, some were advocating for science as a separate discipline, free from religious influence. T.H. Huxley and others seized on the work of Darwin to support an agenda undermining clerical domination of the scientific establishment.

As the nineteenth century progressed, some American writers exploited evolution to promote the idea that science and religion were at war with each other. John William Draper falsely claimed in *History of the Conflict between Religion and Science* that the church had always been opposed to scientific breakthroughs and developments. The book, published in 1872, went through fifty printings and was translated into ten languages.[6]

---

5. Collins, *Language of God*, 200–201.

6. Larsen, "War Is Over," 147–55. "The so-called 'war' between faith and learning, specifically between orthodox Christian theology and science, was manufactured during

Personal

In an effort to distinguish science from religion, some advocates for science over religion suggest that science deals only with facts, observations, and experiment, while religion deals only with mystery, faith, and human experience. That is an over-simplification, of course, since true religion is based on the facts of history, and science is essentially a human endeavor. Observation and experience are common to each.

Science and religion do employ different methods of exploration, however, and their methods complement each other.

God Revealed in Science and Faith

> [Maxwell's work was the] most profound and the most fruitful that physics has experienced since the time of Newton.
>
> —Albert Einstein

James Clerk Maxwell was the greatest physicist of the nineteenth century. He is best known for synthesizing mysteries of electricity, magnetism, and light into a single theory of electromagnetic fields.

Maxwell was a student of the Bible as well as nature, and he found no conflict between the two. As a devout Scottish Presbyterian, he echoed Calvin and Augustine in believing that God was revealed in both the general revelation of nature and the special revelation of the Bible. In other words, all truth is God's truth.

Maxwell found freedom in his Calvinistic faith to explore nature without presuppositions:

> Now my great plan, which was conceived of old ... is to let nothing be willfully left unexamined. Nothing is to be holy ground consecrated to Stationary Faith, whether positive or negative. All fallow land is to be ploughed up and a regular system of rotation followed ... Never hide anything, be it weed or no, nor seem to wish it hidden ... Again I assert the Right of Trespass on any plot of Holy Ground which any man has set apart ... Christianity—that is, the religion of the Bible—is the only scheme or form of belief which disavows any possessions on such a tenure. Here alone all is free. You may fly to the ends of the world and find no God but the

---

the second half of the nineteenth century. It is a construct that was created for polemical purposes."

Author of Salvation. You may search the Scriptures and not find a text to stop you in your explorations...[7]

In the worldview of classical science, God can be envisioned as the Designer and Sustainer of a universe functioning by the laws of nature. Yet the unbending consistency of the laws of nature might seem to constrain God's freedom to act in a universe operating according to his invariant laws.

Envisioning a Personal God in the Worldview of Quantum Mystery

> I cannot conceive of a personal god who would directly influence the actions of individuals... I cannot do this in spite of the fact that mechanistic causality has, to a certain extent, been placed in doubt by modern science. My religiosity consists in a humble admiration of the infinitely superior spirit that reveals itself in the little that we, with our weak and transitory understanding, can comprehend of reality.[8]
>
> —Albert Einstein

Einstein was born in 1879, and he was steeped in the worldview of classical science. Classical science was built on "mechanistic causality," the assumption that, if an experiment is repeated, it always yields the same result.

The marvelous structure of the universe created a religious feeling of awe in Einstein, and he used religious language like "the infinitely superior spirit" or "the old one" to describe the fundamental patterns of the universe that inspired such awe.[9] Yet Einstein's faith in the mechanistic causality of nature made belief in a personal God difficult. The laws of nature, as he understood them, left little space for a personal God to act.

By the 1920s, cracks were appearing in the "mechanistic causality" of classical science. Einstein's "modern science" was quantum mechanics, which injected an element of indeterminacy into the laws of nature at the quantum level. Quantum mechanics challenged Einstein's belief that the laws of nature left no room for a personal God.

---

7. Hutchinson, "James Clerk Maxwell."
8. Dukas and Hoffman, *Albert Einstein: The Human Side*, 66.
9. Polkinghorne, *Science and the Trinity*, 93.

Personal

The Mystery of Indeterminacy

> Quantum mechanics is certainly imposing. But an inner voice tells me that it is not yet the real thing. The theory says a lot, but does not really bring us any closer to the secret of the "old one." I, at any rate, am convinced that he does not throw dice.
>
> —Albert Einstein, 1926

As an example of quantum mechanics, consider an atom in an upper energy level at the center of a spherical fluorescent detector. The atom emits a single photon, which is detected at a particular point on the sphere. Each point has the same probability of being the place where the photon appears.

The experiment follows the rules of quantum mechanics; the emission of the photon is consistent with the energy level of the atom, and the location at which it is detected is consistent with the quantum wave function of the emitted photon. (See Chapter 1.) Yet it is impossible—theoretically impossible—to predict exactly where the photon will be detected, and if the experiment is repeated, the photon will likely be detected at a different location each time.

What determines the particular location where the photon is detected? Since the outcome appears to be random, Einstein flippantly compared the unknown factor in quantum indeterminacy to the chance involved in throwing dice. Yet chance has little to do with causality, and chance in dice is qualitatively different from chance in quantum mechanics.

Chance in dice is determined by *unknown conditions* of the throw, the dice, and the table; theoretically, the mystery of chance could be penetrated by very advanced observations and calculations. Chance in quantum indeterminacy is determined by *unknowable conditions* of the quantum state; it is theoretically impossible to penetrate the mystery and predict the outcome, no matter how advanced the instruments and techniques.

The mysteries of quantum theory generate questions and speculation about the causes of quantum behavior. Is the outcome of the experiment guided by a hidden, undetectable force? Does human consciousness of the outcome extend back in time to direct the path of the photon from the atom to its point of observation? Is detection merely a glimpse into a much larger reality that exists in other dimensions or other universes?

One hundred years after Einstein, the mystery of "the old one" connecting quantum indeterminacy to observable reality is unsolved. Some theories are less reasonable than others: A theory involving a guy named Bob in Pittsburgh should not be considered seriously, and a theory contradicting experimentally-verified probabilities must be rejected.

Space for a Personal God

Einstein resisted quantum mechanics for over twenty years. His objection was not that it seemed strange; he readily embraced strange concepts, such as relativity and warped space-time. Quantum mechanics threatened his worldview, because it created an impenetrable mystery—a gap in causality, inaccessible to human perception. He also recognized the possibility that the mysteries of quantum indeterminacy might create space for a personal God to intervene in nature, without contradicting its laws.

The person-ality of God cannot be confirmed by penetrating quantum mysteries to "catch God in the act" of manipulating the realm of quantum mystery. A theory of a personal God is tested in a different way, suggested by the way in which theories of impenetrable quantum mystery are evaluated in quantum physics.

Evaluating a Quantum Theory: The Higgs Boson

> When physicists in the 1960s modeled behavior of fundamental particles using equations rooted in quantum physics, they encountered a puzzle. If they imagined that the particles were massless, then each term in the equations clicked into a perfectly symmetrical pattern . . . It explained patterns evident in the experimental data. But physicists knew that particles did have mass, and when they modified the equations to account for this fact . . . the equations become complex, unwieldy, and inconsistent.[10]

Fundamental particles, such as quarks, leptons, and bosons, are one hundred million times smaller than an atom and cannot be "seen" directly. They are described by mathematical models, which correspond to experimental observations. Since the equations that modeled quantum behavior in the 1960s did not account for the observable reality of mass, either the equations were wrong, or something was missing from the model.

10. Greene, "How the Higgs Boson Was Found."

Personal

In 1964, Peter Higgs proposed a theory: Quantum theory would be consistent with the reality of mass if there were an undiscovered field permeating the universe, giving mass to particles accelerating through it. The field was named the Higgs field, with the particle designated as the Higgs boson. The popular press picked up the idea that the Higgs boson brought mass into existence, and they called it "The God Particle."

The theory was an elegant solution to a quantum mystery, but no experimental evidence pointed to the existence of the Higgs field. The theory suggested that, under conditions of extremely high energy, a Higgs boson might flash into existence before degenerating into other subatomic particles.

The Higgs theory generated great interest among scientists, and many theoretical physicists accepted it as an *effective* theory.[11] Since it effectively explained the relationship between fundamental particles and measurable mass, it became a key component of the Standard Model of Particle Physics.

Almost fifty years later, the ten billion dollar Large Hadron Collider was constructed at CERN in Switzerland. Scientists used the LHC in 2012 to conduct a high-energy experiment that detected fundamental particles consistent with the predictions of the Higgs theory. The theory was *validated* by experimental confirmation of its predictions.

Evaluating a Theory of Unseen Reality

Significantly, the Higgs boson cannot be "seen" or directly detected, even under high-energy conditions. Yet the Higgs theory is accepted by most scientists, because it is *effective* in explaining the existence of mass, and because observations so far have *validated* the theory.

This suggests a way of evaluating theories about God. As with the Higgs boson, God's essence cannot be "seen" or directly detected by the human senses. Theories about God or his nature can, however, be evaluated by their *effectiveness* in explaining observable reality, and their *validation* in human experience.

---

11. My use of the term "effective theory" is somewhat different from some scientists. Hawking defines it as "a framework created to model certain observed phenomena without describing in detail all of the underlying processes." In his usage, an effective theory is more a tool of reckoning than a theory (*Grand Design*, 32–33). The Higgs theory describes in detail a hypothetical underlying process, providing an elegant explanation for the observable phenomenon of mass.

A THEORY OF A PERSONAL GOD

Throughout the ages, people have believed in a personal God. Some believe because of the historical records of God's actions in the past or the intricate and fruitful design of the universe. Others believe because of personal encounters with God, or because faith makes their lives better.

Some do not believe in a personal God, perhaps because they do not trust historical accounts or they attribute the elegant design of the universe to impersonal forces or undirected evolutionary processes. Others insist on a personal encounter with God on their own terms.

All people, however, reckon with a common reality: Humans are personal. They have self-consciousness identity. They have free will. They are capable of abstract reflection, such as seeking meaning in life or questioning the future of their existence. They communicate with other persons, make judgments based on reason and values, and act with intentionality.

The reality of human person-ality raises a question: What is the *source* of it? The elements that comprise a human person are not personal; carbon-based compounds do not show any evidence of human traits. Yet humans are personal—at least, I think they are, if we are having this conversation!

While evolutionary processes such as natural selection and social evolution might provide mechanisms for human life and consciousness, they do not explain how humans began to ask questions like, "Why am I here?" or "What is the meaning of life?" As Stephen Hawking asked of one aspect of person-ality, "If we have free will, where in the evolutionary tree did it develop?"[12]

Impersonal forces, such as blind chance, life principles, or Einstein's "old one," are unlikely to generate person-ality, which they themselves lack. An alternative theory that humanity generated its own person-ality, by selecting a pathway from all possible quantum histories and evolutionary pathways, is based on circular logic.

The simplest theory is:

The source of human person-ality is a personal God.

If the theory seems contrived, it is no more speculative than theories of unseen quantum forces or particles, which are accepted because they make sense of observable reality. In a similar vein, C.S. Lewis says, "I believe in

---

12. Hawking and Mlodinow, *Grand Design*, 31.

Personal

Christianity as I believe that the Sun has risen, not only because I see it, but because by it, I see everything else."[13]

A theory of a personal God as the source of human person-ality can be tested, as theories of unseen reality are, by its *effectiveness* in providing a foundation for human person-ality. If it proves to be effective, it can then be *validated* by further experiment.

Since human person-ality is complex and multifaceted, this chapter will focus on three facets of person-ality. (A fourth, free will, will be considered in the next chapter.) Humans are characterized by:

1. Purpose
2. Love
3. Enduring Self-Identity

1. Purpose

> I don't feel frightened by not knowing things, by being lost in a mysterious universe without any purpose, which is the way it really is, as far as I can tell. Possibly. It doesn't frighten me.[14]
>
> —Richard P. Feynman

Humans have a unique ability to ask questions about their purpose. As far as we know, dogs and cats do not ask why they exist or whether their actions have significance.

Humans provide purpose for inanimate objects. I read this week about a computer that can play an old video game, *Space Invaders*. Not only can the computer respond quickly, but it can learn strategies and even generate new ones. That causes us to wonder: What is the purpose of a computer competing against a computer? Do the computers care who wins? If there were no humans to care about the games, would they have any purpose? With the right programming and artificial intelligence, it might be possible for computers to generate human-sounding statements about purpose. However, in the absence of humans, would those purpose statements have any meaning?

13. Lewis, "Is Theology Poetry?" 140.
14. Sykes, *No Ordinary Genius*, 239.

Who or what gives purpose to human life?

> If you ask for the purpose or goal of society as a whole or an individual taken as a whole the question loses its meaning... it seems quite arbitrary if not unreasonable to assume somebody whose desires are connected with the happenings. Nevertheless we all feel that it is indeed very reasonable and important to ask ourselves how we should try to conduct our lives. The answer is, in my opinion: satisfaction of the desires and needs of all, as far as this can be achieved, and achievement of harmony and beauty in the human relationships.[15]
>
> —Albert Einstein

Einstein recognized that any purpose or goal of human life would have to be determined by "*somebody*"—some personal entity—for purpose to be a meaningful concept. Since he did not believe in a personal God, he did not believe any ultimate purpose could be determined.

Still, Einstein recognized that humans need a sense of purpose, and he gave his opinion about the goals or objectives of human life: satisfying the needs and desires of all, and achieving harmony and beauty in relationships. Einstein implied that purposeful living is possible, even in the absence of an ultimate purpose for life.

But why should people live as Einstein suggested, and not some other way? Einstein valued human life for all, but his contemporary, Adolf Hitler, did not. Some people value personal freedom over harmony. Some place high value on being a caring person, while others place more value on avoiding shame to themselves and their families. Some aim at nothing more than to be happy and avoid suffering. If the question of purpose is meaningless, why value one goal over another?

Values and goals reflect basic assumptions about the purpose of life. Einstein's goals reflected his assumption that the purpose of life includes enriching life for all, harmony, and beauty. But what if the purpose of life is enriching the gene pool through survival of the fittest or radical individualism? In that case, Einstein's goals do not make sense. Yet if there is no "someone" to determine the ultimate purpose of life, who can say that one purpose is better than another?

---

15. Dukas, *Albert Einstein: The Human Side*, 26–27.

Personal

Does the Nature of Humanity Reveal the Purpose of Life?

> We are just a little advanced breed of monkeys on a small planet orbiting around a very average star. But we can understand the universe, and that makes us very special.[16]
>
> —Stephen Hawking

> A universe without purpose should neither depress us nor suggest that our lives are purposeless. Through an awe-inspiring cosmic history we find ourselves on this remote planet in a remote corner of the universe, endowed with intelligence and self-awareness. We should not despair, but should humbly rejoice in making the most of these gifts, and celebrate our brief moment in the sun.[17]
>
> —Lawrence Krauss

It is reasonable to assume that human gifts and abilities might point to a purpose for human existence. A flower is beautiful and a cow is able to give milk; we assume their purpose relates to their abilities. Humans have intelligence and self-awareness; maybe their purpose is simply to maximize the potential of those abilities.

Yet what is the ultimate purpose of fulfilling human potential? Is a flower beautiful if no one knows the meaning of beauty? If a man runs a record-breaking race and dies at the finish line without anyone knowing, what meaning does that have?

Humans can celebrate, as Krauss suggested, "our brief moment in the sun," but if no one will remain to celebrate after the sun burns out, what enduring purpose does our brief moment have?

The question of purpose is meaningless without an enduring "somebody" who cares about what happens.

---

16. Hawking, interview in *Der Spiegel* (October 17, 1988).
17. Krauss, "Unlikely."

God through Cosmic Lenses

God's Glory Elevates Human Purpose

> What is the chief end of man? Man's chief end is
> to glorify God, and to enjoy him forever.[18]
>
> —WESTMINSTER SHORTER CATECHISM, 1647

In the late 1660s, Sir Christopher Wren was commissioned to redesign St. Paul's Cathedral in London. A legend says that he visited the construction site of this great edifice, unrecognized by the workers. As he walked about the site, he asked several of the men what they were doing. One worker replied, "I am cutting a piece of stone." A second worker responded, "I'm earning five shillings two pence a day." A third, however, said proudly, "I am helping Christopher Wren build a magnificent cathedral to the glory of God."

Personally, I have no desire to work on cathedrals. At lunch today, I shoveled some snow, set out frozen Italian sausage for dinner, and went back to writing. What was the purpose of all of that activity? The snow will eventually melt, my wife would have prepared dinner, and I cannot be sure this book will ever make its way into print. Do everyday actions have purpose?

The catechism says the chief end or purpose of humanity is to glorify God, and Christians believe their actions reflect God's glory. Shoveling snow can reflect God's provision for the needs of people who come to the door, cooking dinner can demonstrate the love of God as it shown in marriage, and writing a book might help someone discover the glory and goodness of God.

Humanity's Role in God's Glorious Creation

> LORD, our Lord, how majestic is your name in all the earth!
>
> You have set your glory in the heavens . . .
>
> When I consider your heavens, the work of your fingers,
>
> the moon and the stars, which you have set in place,
>
> what is mankind that you are mindful of them,
> human beings that you care for them?
>
> You have made them a little lower than the angels

---

[18] *Westminster Shorter Catechism*, Q. 1.

> and crowned them with glory and honor.
>
> You made them rulers over the works of your
> hands; you put everything under their feet:
>
> all flocks and herds, and the animals of the wild,
> the birds of the air, and the fish of the sea.
>
> —Psalm 8:1–8

Considering all that is now known about the universe, a modern writer might have even more reason for awe than the ancient writer of the psalm. Although humans are specks of dust in an awesome universe, God bestows *glory and honor* on them as rulers over creation. The doctor who cures disease, the gardener who grows food or creates a beautiful landscape, the fisherman who practices sustainable harvesting, and the old woman who lovingly takes care of her cat—all are fulfilling a glorious purpose given by God.

Reflecting God's Glory in Godly Character

> And we, who with unveiled faces all reflect the Lord's glory,
> are being transformed into his likeness with ever-increasing
> glory, which comes from the Lord, who is the Spirit.
>
> —2 Corinthians 3:18

Unlike robots, which are created for what they can *do*, humans are created for what they can *be* as well as *do*. They can reflect the glory of God by their character!

My mother, as many women in her generation, did not work outside the home. Some would say she lived in the shadow of her husband, although her children know otherwise. When she died, her obituary did not include earning a PhD, building a mathematics department, or touching the lives of thousands of students. Yet those who knew her saw the glory of God reflected in her character, even until she died at age ninety-five.

By nature, every person reflects the glory of God in some way. Yet those who know the grace of God through Jesus Christ grow in their ability to reflect God's glory. As a traditional funeral prayer says: "For all that she was, by nature and by grace, we give you thanks."

Sharing in God's Glorious Plan

> God made known to us the mystery of his will ... which he purposed in Christ, to be put into effect when the times will have reached their fulfillment—to bring unity to all things in heaven and on earth under Christ. In him we were also chosen, having been predestined according to the plan of him who works out everything in conformity with the purpose of his will, in order that we, who were the first to put our hope in Christ, might be for the praise of his glory.
>
> —Ephesians 1:9–12

Would you like to have as much impact on human history as Albert Einstein? His contributions to human knowledge are celebrated a century later. Without Einstein, there might not have been ... an atomic bomb dropped on Hiroshima! Einstein deeply regretted the use of his discoveries to build a bomb, and he had a rather idealistic hope that someday the world would swear off the use of force.

We all leave a legacy, and we would like its impact to be good as well as lasting. Without God, our legacy will be limited by the imperfection of the world, as well as the eventual demise of the universe.

The Bible presents a more optimistic prospect: God will redeem the universe, weaving it into a larger reality ruled by Christ. The apostle Paul calls this a "mystery" of God's will, since it goes beyond the universe and is beyond comprehension. The glory of this mystery, for those who accept it, is that they have a place in God's glorious purpose. It is possible, even in a life that seems insignificant, to contribute to God's perfect plan for all ages!

A Personal God as an Effective Source of Purpose

Belief in a personal God provides a foundation for human purpose, beyond fulfilling human potential. The purpose of human life is to glorify God.

2. Love

Love may be the highest trait of human person-ality. Individuals are defined, to a large degree, by what and whom they love, and how they love.

Yet it is more difficult than some might think to say what love is, where it comes from, and what makes human love so amazing.

People think of love as a personal choice, but is it totally a choice? We once had a dog that seemed to love me because I fed her and took her out for exercise; our cat, which I sometimes not-too-gently pushed out the door with my foot, seemed not to love me as much. Is love merely a conditioned response, or can human love be deeper than that?

Love Arising from Undirected Evolutionary Processes

> I don't want you to love me for qualities you assume in me . . . in fact not for any qualities; you must love me as irrationally as other people love, just because I love you, and you don't have to be afraid of it.[19]
>
> —SIGMUND FREUD TO MARTHA BERNAYS

What causes people to love?

Evolutionary biology explains love in terms of natural selection. When the female of the species seeks a mate, she looks for a dominant male, strong and healthy, able to protect and provide. The male looks for a healthy female, able to bear healthy offspring that will improve his genetic lines.

Deep in the prehistory of humans, a male impregnates a female. By some genetic or environmental accident, he does not abandon her or treat her as just another conquest, but stays with her, showing her preferential treatment. She likes the way he treats her, and encourages further preferential treatment by catering to his desires. Her children have the advantage of the protection and skills of a male, and they learn the advantages of choosing a mate and staying together. Because of their advantages, the family thrives, while other families are less successful and eventually die out. A pattern of mutual benefit and pleasure develops, which people call love.

Love of this sort contributes to natural selection; it promotes the fitness of the individual, and survives through genetic and social selection.

How then does one explain unselfish love? A warrior on the battlefield sacrifices his life for his brothers in combat. It is hard to see natural selection at work in his sacrifice, since by his act of selflessness the warrior has lost his ability to sire children. Maybe, though, if enough warriors in his tribal group sacrifice their lives for others, the group will thrive, destroying

---

19. O'Neill, *Freud and the Passions*, 9.

other more selfish groups. Unselfish love then provides evolutionary advantage, establishing it as a group value.

Merely Animal Instinct?

> How do I love thee? Let me count the ways.
> I love thee to the depth and breadth and height
> My soul can reach, when feeling out of sight
> For the ends of being and ideal grace.
> I love thee to the level of every day's
> Most quiet need, by sun and candle-light.
> I love thee freely, as men strive for right.
> I love thee purely, as they turn from praise.
> I love thee with the passion put to use
> In my old griefs, and with my childhood's faith.
> I love thee with a love I seemed to lose
> With my lost saints. I love thee with the breath,
> Smiles, tears, of all my life; and, if God choose,
> I shall but love thee better after death.[20]
>
> —Elizabeth Barrett Browning

The evolutionary origin of love explains a lot, although it does take away some of the wonder of love poems. The joy and power of human love is that it rises above animal instinct, freely seeking higher ideals of grace and permanence.

Evolutionary advantage does not always generate love in the animal kingdom. Weak or infirm animals are often killed or abandoned. Offspring of other males, or sometimes females, are either neglected or attacked.

Human behavior sometimes displays the same destructive animal instincts. Eugenics, presented as a way to improve the gene pool, prepared the way for Nazi genocide. Discrimination based on racial or socioeconomic

---

20 Browning, "Sonnet 43."

Personal

status can be weaponized to protect the advantages of a dominant group. Value or influence can depend upon physical attractiveness, power, or wealth.

Yet many humans display love that goes beyond animal instincts. Couples marry, vowing to be faithful "in sickness and in health." Parents continue to love their children, even when children are lost to drugs or crime. People care for handicapped children, foster children, or feeble parents, at great personal cost. They give money to feed hungry children and dig wells in far-off places, in communities they will never visit. The evolutionary advantage of those actions is far from clear, especially regarding individuals whose survival adds little to the individual or larger social group.

Sacrificial Love

During World War II, the *USAT Dorchester* left New York, carrying about nine hundred U.S. troops and crew and four chaplains: two Protestant, one Catholic, and one Jewish. A German U-Boat torpedoed the ship, and panic set in. The chaplains sought to calm the men and organize an orderly evacuation of the ship, guiding wounded men to safety. When the supply of life jackets ran out, the chaplains removed their own life jackets and gave them to others. After helping as many men as possible into lifeboats, they linked arms, praying and singing hymns, until the ship went down. Why did they do that? Were their actions based on some vestige of evolutionary sociobiology, or were they motivated by something more?

Love in the Image of God

> Man in Scripture is much more than homo faber, the maker of tools: he is constituted man by God's image and breath, nothing less... Nothing requires that the creature into which God breathed human life should not have been of a species prepared in every way for humanity, with already a long history of practical intelligence, artistic sensibility and the capacity for awe and reflection.[21]
>
> —Derek Kidner

---

21. Kidner says, "It follows that Scripture and science may well differ in the boundaries they would draw around early humanity: the intelligent beings of a remote past, whose bodily and cultural remains give them the clear status of 'modern man' to the anthropologist, may yet have been decisively below the plane of life which was established

Contrary to some interpretations, the Bible does not deny that humans evolved from other human-like creatures. However, Genesis insists that the source of humanity is not evolution *alone*. Humans receive their identity from God himself, who says, "Let us make man in our image..."

It would not be wrong to say that the most essential element of the image of God is the ability to love God and other people in a way that reflects the love of God. Humans have a source of love beyond what they inherit from millennia of evolutionary and social development.

God Is Love: The Trinity

> Now this is the catholic faith:
>
> That we worship one God in trinity and the trinity in unity,
>
> neither blending their persons nor dividing their essence.
>
> For the person of the Father is a distinct person,
>
> the person of the Son is another,
>
> and that of the Holy Spirit still another.
>
> But the divinity of the Father, Son, and Holy Spirit is one.[22]
>
> —Athanasian Creed, AD 500

The doctrine of the Trinity encapsulates a paradox found in the Bible: God is one, and yet he is encountered distinctly as Father, Son, and Holy Spirit. Creeds like the Athanasian Creed seek to resolve the paradox by carefully chosen words and definitions.

Definitions cannot capture the deepest mystery, however. God's essential nature is not solitary; it incorporates a deep and abiding love between Father, Son, and Holy Spirit. Jesus said the Father loves the Son, and the Son loves the Father. The Holy Spirit brings glory to the Son, and they freely share everything.[23] The lifeblood of the Trinity is love.

---

in the creation of Adam. If, as the text of Genesis would by no means disallow, God initially shaped man by a process of evolution, it would follow that a considerable stock of near-humans preceded the first true man, and it would be arbitrary to picture these as mindless brutes." (*Genesis*, 28).

22. Translation, Christian Reformed Church of North America, 1988.

23. 1 John 4:16, John 3:35, 14:31, 16:14–15.

Personal

The love of God spills over toward humanity, uniquely expressed by each of God's three persons. The Father loved the world so much that he sent his beloved Son to save. The Son showed his love in the person of Jesus, who gave his life for his friends.[24] The Holy Spirit brings the reality of God's love into the hearts of believers.[25] There is no need to resolve the mystery of the Trinity to accept the love of the Father, Son, and Holy Spirit; it is one love, personally expressed.

God's Circle of Love

> When Israel was a child, I loved him . . . I led them
> with cords of human kindness, with ties of love.
>
> —HOSEA 11:1–4

My parents loved each other. That would have been a source of strength and stability for me, even if I had not lived with them. But I did live with them, and their love enfolded me! My brother, sister, and I were included in their circle of their love, and it made us who we are today.

The love at the core of the Trinity is a source of stability for God's children, and the greatest wonder of God's love is that people can be included within the circle of love.

The biblical story begins with two humans in the circle of God's love. Adam and Eve were secure in the love of God, and because of that, they were secure in their relationships with the world and with each other. When they rebelled against God, doubting his love, they experienced fear, shame, and broken relationships.

The Old Testament continues the story, as God brings people back into the circle of his love. He reaches out to Abraham and his descendants, enfolding them in a covenant of love and faithfulness. When people failed to keep the covenant, God refuses to give up on them.

The New Testament reveals how God expands the circle of his covenant love to include all people. Through Jesus, all people gain access to the Father, and all who accept his invitation enter the circle of God's love. The language of the New Testament is striking: It is the language of adoption, inclusion, and entering into a life-giving relationship with God. In

---

24. John 15:12–13.
25. John 3:16, John 15:12–13, Rom 5:5.

the circle of God's love, the love of Father, Son, and Holy Spirit is shared, as described in Galatians 4:6: "Because you are his sons, God sent the Spirit of his Son into our hearts, the Spirit who calls out, 'Abba, Father.'"

Expanding the Circle

> I kneel before the Father, from whom every concept and experience of fatherhood in the universe is named.[26]
>
> —EPHESIANS 3:14–15

> Husbands, love your wives, just as Christ loved the church and gave himself up for her.
>
> —EPHESIANS 5:25

> Dear friends, let us love one another, for love comes from God. Everyone who loves has been born of God and knows God . . . Since God so loves us, we also ought to love one another.
>
> —1 JOHN 4:7, 11

God's love enables people to love spouses, children, friends, and even needy strangers. Although human love is imperfect, God's love redeems and restores the human capacity to love.

God's love is not motivated by self-interest or evolutionary advantage. The New Testament writers adopted a rare Greek word for love, *agape*, to make clear that the love of those who know God goes beyond sexual and reproductive desire (*eros*, erotic love) or the love of family or friends (*philia*, filial love).

The early church grew because Christians reflected the self-giving love of God in caring for the sick, risking their lives for people beyond their family circles. Throughout history, Christians have expressed God's love in giving to the poor, educating children, establishing hospitals, and standing for justice, even when they gained no personal advantage from doing so.

---

26. My translation, based on Francis Foulkes, *Epistle of Paul to the Ephesians*, 101.

Personal

A Personal God as an Effective Source of Love

Belief in a personal God provides a solid and noble foundation for human love. Other theories about God fall short of explaining the beauty and kindness of the highest forms of human love, and give little motivation for people to pursue love unselfishly. It is not without reason that the Bible says, "God is love."

3. Enduring Self-Identity

I was seated in an airplane when I started to write this section. For some reason, I began to think about what would happen to me if the plane crashed and I died. There would be three possibilities:

- I would immediately cease to exist, in which case I would live constantly on the edge of non-being. My memory would live on in the minds of certain people, until they also died.
- My "soul" would not die, but would live on—either in a disembodied state, or migrating to a new body through reincarnation or transmigration.
- God, who knows and loves me now, would cause me to live on, giving me an enduring spiritual existence that would be truly "me."

Neither of the first two possibilities necessarily assume a personal God, because they are based on whether humans have (or are essentially) an immortal soul that lives beyond death. The third possibility depends entirely on a personal God.

Can Consciousness Exist Apart from the Body?

> While the neurons of my cortex were stunned to complete inactivity by the bacteria that had attacked them, my brain-free consciousness journeyed to another, larger dimension of the universe.[27]
>
> —Eben Alexander, MD

---

27. Alexander, *"Proof of Heaven."*

Dr. Alexander's book generated considerable discussion about whether humans might have an immortal soul or spirit that could live apart from body and mind. It is impossible to know, of course, whether his memories were from an experience outside of his body or generated in his brain as he slipped in and out of consciousness.

There is no scientific reason to believe that consciousness can exist apart from the brain. Nobel laureate Roger Sperry asserts, "Everything in science to date seems to indicate that conscious awareness is a property of the brain and inseparable from it."[28] Yet belief in the possibility of conscious existence apart from the brain and body persists. What is the origin of that idea?

The concept of the soul existing apart from the body was foreign to the Old Testament, as the Hebrew word for soul (*nephesh*) referred to the whole being of animals as well as people. The concept was common in Greek culture, however. Plato said, "Do we believe that there is such a thing as death? . . . Is it not the separation of soul and body? And to be dead is the completion of this; when the soul exists in herself, and is released from the body and the body is released from the soul, what is this but death?"[29]

The New Testament writers adopted the language of their culture, and they referred to body, soul, and spirit, while maintaining the unity of person-ality.[30] The apostle Paul recognized the ethical dangers of too great a distinction between soul and body, as deeds done in the body might then be irrelevant to the life of the soul. He argued that deeds done in the body have spiritual significance.[31]

In later centuries, some influential Christian writers adopted the language and concepts of soul-body duality. The idea of the soul existing apart from the body persists, although the Bible teaches something quite different.

An Identity Secure in God

> I adore you, sweetheart. I know how much you like to hear that . . .
> You only are left to me. You are real. My darling wife, I do adore
> you. I love my wife. My wife is dead. Rich. P.S. Please excuse

---

28. Quoted in Myers, *Friendly Letter*, 27–28.
29. Plato, *Five Dialogues*, 94.
30. 1 Thess 5:23, Heb 4:12.
31. 1 Cor 6:12–20.

Personal

> my not mailing this—but I don't know your new address.[32]
>
> —Richard P. Feynman

> For you died, and your life is now hidden with Christ
> in God. When Christ, who is your life, appears,
> then you also will appear with him in glory.
>
> —Colossians 3:3–4

When people die, we might say they continue to live in the memory of those who loved them. We understand that the memory is a mere shadow of the life that once was, and when the ones who loved them die, their memory also dies.

When Christians die, they live on in God's memory, which never dies. Yet God's memory is more than a shadow from the past; it is the basis of a new reality that endures forever.

New Bodies

> I declare to you, brothers, that flesh and blood cannot inherit the
> kingdom of God, nor does the perishable inherit the imperishable.
> Listen, I tell you a mystery: We will not all sleep, but we will all
> be changed—in a flash, in the twinkling of an eye, at the last
> trumpet. For the trumpet will sound, the dead will be raised
> imperishable, and we will be changed. For the perishable must
> clothe itself with the imperishable, and the mortal with immortality.
> When the perishable has been clothed with the imperishable,
> and the mortal with immortality, then the saying that is written
> will come true: "Death has been swallowed up in victory."
>
> —1 Corinthians 15:50–54

If human person-ality is joined to a mortal body before death, it would be strange for it to be disembodied after death. The New Testament indicates that the essential person-ality of believers will reside in a new body when the old one is dead and gone.

---

32. Gleick, *Genius*, 222.

Resurrected bodies are not like earthly bodies, however. The apostle Paul compares the physical body to a seed that is planted, dying to be reborn into something more glorious. He says God will clothe the person-ality of believers in a new body, which will be powerful, immortal, and spiritual.

Although resurrected bodies will be new, God will give them the identity of the person who lived on earth. Personal identity will be renewed and perfected, in a new and more lasting form.

The Best Self

> The Lord Jesus Christ... will transform our lowly bodies so that they will be like his glorious body.
>
> —PHILIPPIANS 3:20–21

My older cousin, Johnny, had limited mental capacity, and I remember him paging through the same magazines over and over again, viewing the pictures with a perpetual smile on his face. Johnny's greatest contribution on the family farm was that he could scoop chicken manure for hours without feeling bored or dissatisfied.

Johnny's parents taught him about Jesus, and a time came when he met with the elders of the church to declare his faith, simply mumbling, "I love Jesus." He loved people too, and I remember him at the coffin of my grandpa, saying with great emotion, "Sampa." He was, in his own way, a remarkable person.

Johnny died a few years ago, and I am sure his body and mind are glorious, putting my earthly body to shame! Yet Johnny is still the same Johnny, who loved Jesus and loved Grandpa.

A Personal God as an Effective Source of Personal Identity

Without a personal God, enduring self-identity depends upon unproven and shadowy theories of human personhood separate from physical existence. These theories fall short of corresponding to the scientific reality of human person-ality residing in the brain, yet enduring beyond death.

A theory of a personal God grounds enduring self-identity in the memory of God and the power of God to preserve human person-ality in

Personal

a new form. Faith in a God who remembers provides a more solid foundation for believing that human identity endures.

Validating the Theory by Experience

Scientific theories are validated by *experimental* confirmation. A ball drops in a vacuum, as the law of gravity predicts. An object moving through a magnetic field produces an electrical current, and the measurement is consistent with Maxwell's equations. Mixing two chemicals produces the predicted compound.

Theories involving people are not as easy to test by experimental means, because human personality is exceedingly complex. Even experiments in the social sciences, which control for human factors, are unavoidably tied to human experience.

While *experiment* and *experience* share the same linguistic root, experiment implies that the observer is irrelevant, while experience requires participation. Ultimately, the person-ality of God is validated in experience, both individual and collective. People are unavoidably participants in testing the theory of a personal God.

A Personal Experiment

> An "impersonal God"—well and good ... But God himself alive ...
> That is quite another matter ... There comes a moment when
> people who have been dabbling in religion ("man's search for God"!)
> suddenly draw back. Supposing we really found Him? We never
> meant it to come to that! Worse still, supposing He had found us?[33]
>
> —C.S. Lewis

Many scientific theories can be evaluated without personal investment. Either the universe contains dark matter, or it doesn't; the sun will rise tomorrow. Either life exists on other planets, or it doesn't; the theory doesn't matter, unless a UFO visits the earth.

The theory of a personal God is quite different, because it inevitably affects the way people live.

---

33. Lewis, *Miracles*, 96–97.

God through Cosmic Lenses

Consider this mystery: A young woman opens her apartment door one morning to find a dozen roses. No one knows how the roses got there, but she may have a theory. If she has a boyfriend, he is a likely candidate. If she gave her address to a stranger at a party last night, he might be the prime suspect. If she is a secret agent or her friends like pranks, she might have other theories. Of course, it could be that someone left the roses at the wrong apartment. Each theory might impact her life in significant ways, and she is personally involved in exploring the truth. She can test her theory by further experience—exploring her theory and discovering what it entails.

Investigating whether God is personal is never merely an intellectual exercise. It entails a personal quest for purpose, love, and enduring self-identity, with profound personal implications.

Infinitely Personal

THE PREVIOUS TWO CHAPTERS described God as *Infinite* and *Personal*. Envisioning God as *Infinitely Personal* offers fresh perspectives on age-old mysteries of prayer, miracles, and free will.

PRAYER AND A PERSONAL RELATIONSHIP WITH GOD

An inquisitive child praying the Lord's Prayer sincerely asked, "Our Father who art in heaven, how do you know my name?" That is a good question! With billions of people in the world, how can God know each one *personally*? Does he employ a massive database? Is he an accomplished multitasker, who gives each person a sliver of his attention? Or is the idea that God knows people personally just wishful thinking?

Relationships of Finite Person-ality

How many friends do you have? Not just friends or followers on social media, but friends you talk with, friends you care about personally, friends you can count on. We might know hundreds of people, but we have neither the time nor emotional energy to have close relationships with all of them.

If we imagine that God is limited to finite person-ality, we can hardly think of him as more than an acquaintance. We might check in with him occasionally, and he might follow our progress with interest, but our relationship will inevitably be distant.

God through Cosmic Lenses

Relationships with an Infinitely Personal God

> I have called you friends... the Father will give you whatever you ask in my name.
>
> —John 15:13–16

Can you imagine a friendship with a famous person? Probably not! Famous people are only human; they have a finite amount of time and attention to give, and you are probably not near the top of their list of potential friends.

God is not limited like that; he is *infinitely personal*. The equation that describes God's interaction with people is wonderfully inexhaustible:

$\infty - x = \infty$, where x is any finite number of people

Since God is infinitely personal, the time and attention he gives to one person does not reduce the time and attention he can give to others. He is able to give every person his full attention, without being distracted by others or checking a screen to keep up on world events.

God's infinite capacity for relationships allows every person to be a "friend" of God. Friends share thoughts and emotions, as well as desires and requests. As my daughter taught me when she was four years old, "Dad, sometimes when you pray, you don't have to ask God for anything. Sometimes you don't have any plans for him."

God and Prayer Requests

In the movie *Bruce Almighty*, Bruce has taken on God's responsibilities for a time. He sits at his computer, answering prayers as they come in from around the world. There are 1,527,503 prayers! He grabs a cup of coffee and gets to work, his fingers flying at superhuman speed across the keyboard to instantaneously answer each prayer in an instant. After several minutes, he checks his progress, only to discover that the number of unanswered prayers has doubled! In desperation, he clicks the button, "Yes to all," with unintended consequences, of course.

How is it possible for God to respond to the prayers of even a thousand people at a time? Does he delegate to his angels, personally handling only the most critical requests? Does a massive supercomputer group requests by topic, so he can consider the ones that pique his interest? Does he give each prayer a microsecond of his attention before moving on to the next pressing need?

It sounds silly, but some prayer practices reflect that kind of thinking. People post requests for prayer on social media, with the idea that a thousand prayers by total strangers will merit God's attention. Some ask saints or angels to intervene, believing that if God doesn't get around to listening to their prayers, he might listen to someone who has a stronger connection to the Almighty. Others hesitate to pray about everyday needs, because they feel God has only enough time to handle more important requests.

Since God is *infinitely personal*, no request is too insignificant for God's consideration. Not only that, but God is able to hear my prayer for rain for the garden and my neighbor's prayer for no rain for a baseball game, and he can answer our prayers in the best possible way.

MIRACLES AND THE LAWS OF NATURE

Children sometimes ask whether there is anything God cannot do. The simple answer is that nothing in nature keeps God from doing what he decides to do. He created the universe and its laws, and he has power over all the forces of nature.

Still, is there anything God cannot do? Actually, there is! God cannot go against his character.[1] God cannot lie, promote evil, fail to love, or tolerate injustice. In regard to the universe, God cannot establish the laws of nature and promise to uphold them and then ignore them as if they did not exist. Doing so would not only make a sham of the laws of nature, but would also be contrary to his truth and faithfulness.

God Upholds the Laws of Nature

> As long as the earth endures, seedtime and harvest, cold and heat, summer and winter, day and night will never cease.
>
> —GENESIS 8:22

---

1. 2 Tim 2:13.

God through Cosmic Lenses

> The LORD does whatever pleases him, in the heavens and on the earth, in the seas and all their depths. He makes clouds rise from the ends of the earth; he sends lightning with the rain and brings out the wind from his storehouses.
>
> —PSALM 135:6–7

The creation story in Genesis is tailored to the worldview of pre-scientific people, but it is in harmony with current scientific theories as it opens with, "In the beginning God created the heavens and the earth. Now the earth was *formless and empty . . .*"

Genesis goes on to assert that God brought form and structure into the universe. The point of the six days of creation is not how many hours it took for God to create the universe, since that was already accomplished in Gen 1:1. As God spoke on the six days, the chaos of the universe conformed to the design of God, and the earth emerged as an orderly environment suitable for life. There was "evening and morning . . . seasons and days and years . . . [sun and moon] to govern the day and night . . . [living things] according to their kinds."

After creation, God promised to uphold the laws of nature.[2] He promised to preserve the seasons and movement of the planets, and Psalm 19 implies that the certainty of the laws of nature declares the glory of God, just as the certainty of the moral law declares his glory.

On the other hand, the Bible indicates that God can act freely. He answers prayers, he does miracles, and he changes the course of history. The laws of nature do not prevent God from intervening in the universe he created.

The biblical accounts present a paradox: God sustains the order of the universe, and yet he acts freely. The paradox is difficult to resolve within the framework of classical science and theology.

Determinism in Classical Science

> We ought to regard the present state of the universe as the effect of its antecedent state and as the cause of the state that is to follow. An intelligence knowing all the forces acting in nature at a given instant, as well as the momentary positions of all things in the

---

2. Gen 8:22; see also Jer 31:35–36.

universe, would be able to comprehend in one single formula the motions of the largest bodies as well as the lightest atoms in the world, provided that its intellect were sufficiently powerful to subject all data to analysis; to it nothing would be uncertain, the future as well as the past would be present to its eyes.[3]

—Pierre Simon Laplace, 1820

Laplace was a famous French scientist and mathematician, best known for defining *scientific determinism*. In modern terms, determinism says that if the initial state of a system is known (including position, momentum, and forces operating in the system) the state of the system thereafter is fully determined by the laws of nature.

Classical science was based on determinism. It assumed that the present state of the universe could be determined with certainty, and therefore the future state of the universe could be determined with certainty. Rigid faith in determinism makes no allowance for God to act or intervene.

Yet, as Laplace pointed out, certainty about the future depends on knowing, with certainty, the positions and forces of nature. Discoveries in the past century raise questions about the possibility of such total certainty.

Quantum Uncertainty

The more precisely the position is determined, the less precisely the momentum is known, in this instant, and vice versa.

—Werner Heisenberg, 1927

A teenager is driving down a highway, and his mother is talking to him on his cell phone. The mother wants to know exactly where he is—which mile marker—and exactly how fast he is driving. The boy politely informs her that he can tell her either one or the other, but not both at the same time. If he looks at the mile marker along the road, he can't read the speedometer accurately; if he looks at the speedometer, he can't see the mile marker clearly. The mother, of course, asks how many beers he has consumed!

One of the key understandings of the quantum world is something like that. The Heisenberg Uncertainty Principle says that the more precisely

---

3. Hoefer, "Causal Determinism."

the position of a particle is known, the less precisely the its momentum can be known. Mathematically, the equation looks like this:

$$\Delta x \Delta p > \frac{h}{2\pi}$$

where Δx is the uncertainty of the position, Δp is the uncertainty of the momentum, and h is Planck's constant, a tiny number (6.63×10^{-34} joule-seconds) that occurs in nature.

As you can imagine, the Heisenberg Uncertainty Principle was not easy to accept. Some scientists argued that every particle does have a precise position and momentum; it is just not possible to determine exactly what it is. Other scientists contended that reality at a quantum level can never be known precisely! That does not seem logical, but most physicists are now convinced that it is true; *uncertainty* is an essential feature of the quantum universe.

We should be careful not to jump to unwarranted conclusions. The position and momentum of a particle can be approximately determined; it is not "maybe here, or maybe in China." The position and momentum of a particle can be precisely described by a quantum field function, which determines the probabilities of both present and future states. Yet the quantum field function allows for degrees of uncertainty that cannot be eliminated.

Quantum uncertainty is intrinsic in the laws of nature at the quantum level, but there is a huge difference between the quantum scale and the scale of everyday life. Can quantum uncertainty affect events on the scale of human experience?

Quantum Impact on a Human Scale

In 1935, Erwin Schrödinger posed a famous thought experiment. A cat is placed in a closed box, which contains a radioactive atom with a fifty-fifty chance of decaying in the next hour, emitting an alpha particle. If a particle is detected by a Geiger counter, a poisonous gas is released, instantly killing the cat. At the end of the hour, an observer lifts the lid of the box, and the cat is determined to be either dead or alive.

The experiment raises a question: "What is the state of the cat while the box is closed?" Since the fate of the cat is linked to quantum uncertainty, some argue that the cat is neither dead nor alive (or both dead and alive!) from the time the box is closed to the time when the human observer sees the cat and determines its state. Others point to the absurdity of that argument: Why should reality depend upon human consciousness rather than cat consciousness? What if, in a twisted perversion of science, the cat is replaced by a child that does not know about the experiment?

Philosophical gymnastics misses the point: Quantum uncertainty can influence events on the scale of human experience! When an alpha particle is emitted and its probability wave function collapses into certainty, the cat also collapses. When the observer opens the box and determines the state of the quantum system, he will either feed the cat or bury it.

If reality at the quantum level is inherently uncertain, and quantum-level events affect events at the level of human experience, human history is open—at least a crack—to uncertainty. This does not necessarily refute faith in determinism, but it requires a modification of classical determinism to allow for uncertainty and alternate histories.

Of course, the experiment depends on a carefully-constructed mechanism to connect small-scale quantum history and large-scale cat history. Does nature provide similar mechanisms?

Chaos Theory

> The idea that the state of the universe at one time determines the state at all other times has been a central tenet of science, ever since Laplace's time. It implies that we can predict the future, in principle at least. In practice, our ability to predict the future is severely limited by the complexity of the equations, and the fact that they often have a property called chaos... a tiny disturbance in one place can cause a major change in another. A butterfly flapping its wings can cause rain in Central Park. The trouble is, it is not repeatable. The next time the butterfly flaps its wings, a host of other things will be different.[4]
>
> —STEPHEN HAWKING

---

4. Hawking, "Does God Play Dice?"

God through Cosmic Lenses

In 1961, meteorologist Edward Lorenz was re-running a computer model to forecast a weather system. To save time, he rounded off one of the variables from .506127 to .506. That tiny change caused a completely different weather scenario. He published his work, but no one paid much attention until, over ten years later, he made the idea visual in a talk titled, *Predictability: Does the Flap of a Butterfly's Wings in Brazil Set Off a Tornado in Texas?*[5] Within a short time, popular culture became enamored with the butterfly effect. A popular expression of the idea is that a random act of kindness might change the course of history, or at least bring together a man and a woman in a romantic comedy.

Chaos theory suggests that tiny changes within a system are magnified in interaction with other forces to produce larger changes. We instinctively recognize how chaos theory works: A mosquito landing on my nose might distract me enough to cause a life-changing accident, or a glitch in the division of the DNA in a brain cell could be the beginning of a cancer that takes my life.

Hawking insists *in principle* that chaos theory does not contradict belief in determinism, but he admits that *in practice* the complexity of the equations (or variables) causing an event makes predicting the future humanly impossible.

God's Freedom within the Laws of Nature

When I was a boy, I spent a week with my cousin on the farm. The summer had been dry, the corn was withering, and the harvest was in danger. I still remember the emotions I felt one night as my cousin and I looked out the window of his upstairs bedroom in the old farmhouse. We heard the rumbling of thunder and saw flashes of lightning, and then we could almost feel the rain pouring onto the thirsty ground. My uncle said it was a million dollar rain, and we believed it was a gift from God.

Could God send rain without breaking the laws of nature that he established? Nature doesn't care whether a butterfly flaps its wings a minute earlier, a volcano blows a day earlier, or the ocean warms two degrees. Some might argue for a kind of determinism that does not allow God to cause such events, but that would be a purely philosophical argument. From a scientific point of view, having a butterfly flap its wings a minute earlier rather than a minute later does nothing to undermine the laws of nature.

5. Dizikes, "Butterfly."

Hawking suggests that predicting the future might be possible, except that the "equations"—or more precisely, the variables and their interactions—are so incredibly complex that events are unpredictable. Changing the future would be even more difficult, since it would require working out all possible histories, assessing their impact, and then acting far in advance of the future outcome. The variations are almost endless—almost—for they are finite.

For God to act freely while upholding the laws of nature, he would need to know all the equations, as well as their solutions. He would need to coordinate probability events within the determinacy of the quantum laws of nature, and fit together all the order and chaos of history to lead to desired consequences.

God's actions would require him to be *infinitely* aware, *infinitely* wise, and *infinitely* powerful. He would also have to be *personally* involved with every aspect of the universe, from beginning to end, with a passionate desire to exercise his freedom of choice while preserving the laws of nature. In a phrase, he would have to be *infinitely personal!*

Types of Miracles

> By definition, miracles must of course interrupt the usual course of Nature; but if they are real, they must, in the very act of so doing, assert the unity and self-consistency of total reality at some deeper level . . . If what we call Nature is modified by supernatural power, then we can be sure that the capability of being so modified is of the essence of Nature.[6]
>
> —C.S. Lewis

If God's freedom is not constrained by the laws of nature, we can envision three kinds of miracles: miracles within the laws of nature, miracles as exceptions to the laws of nature, and miracles obeying higher laws.

Miracles within the Laws of Nature

A miracle need not be contrary to the laws of nature; the miraculous element is that God chooses to work within the indeterminacy of the universe.

---

6. Lewis, *Miracles*, 62–63.

For example, a cancer cell meets up with a T cell, and the body's immune system is unleashed to destroy the cancer and heal the body. The body's immune system is a miracle of God's design, including the original design of the universe, the guidance of God in the formation of life, and the evolutionary process through which it developed. Cancer cells are destroyed without contradicting any laws of nature.

Yet not all cancer cells are destroyed. In fact, there may be a certain probability or indeterminacy about whether cancer cells in a person's body will be destroyed. If someone prays, and God makes a miracle happen, it is not contrary to the laws of nature; it is simply that God (in Hawking's words) "solved the equations or variables" to make the miracle happen in that particular time and place. The variables might include genetic mutations or environmental factors centuries before, the healthy vegetables the person was eating, or the fluid dynamics directing that particular T cell in the blood.

The miracle in this case is not that God contradicts the laws of nature, because nature allows for indeterminacy in these areas. The miracle is that God is able to handle all of the variables, in many times and places, within the laws of nature that he established. A greater miracle is that he cares enough about individual people to do so!

These kinds of miracles might be considered "happy coincidences," and in a sense, they are, as the goodness of God and the needs of people coincide. Recognizing that fact should not lessen one's awe and wonder at miracles, but increase them.

Miracles as Exceptions to the Laws of Nature

Making an exception to a rule is not the same as disregarding the rule. In fact, the very nature of an exception is that the rule remains.

In a miracle, God might take exception to one of the laws of nature. If he did that regularly, nature would no longer be dependable, and science would be almost impossible.

For this reason, exceptions to the laws of nature are rare. When they appear in the Bible, they are a sign of God's power, usually signifying a unique and unusual movement. The ministry of Jesus was characterized by signs, as were the early activities of the church in Acts. Today, sign-miracles appear to be most common among people groups where the gospel is beginning to take hold.

Of course, miracles like this must not throw the entire universe out of sync, so it may be that even when such miracles appear to be exceptions to the laws of nature, God "solves the equations" to allow them to occur without wreaking havoc with the laws of nature.

Miracles Obeying Deeper Laws.

According to C.S. Lewis, miracles "must assert the unity and self-consistency of total reality at some deeper level." If the universe is a subspace of a larger reality, as envisioned in previous chapters, miracles might entail God operating according to higher or deeper laws—supernatural laws.

A simple analogy is a bank account: If I try to withdraw money from my account, I cannot take out more than the account balance. There are rules against that, and if the bank did not follow the rules, it would not be in business very long. However, there are no rules against a rich benefactor depositing money into my account. The benefactor follows a set of rules beyond the realm of my bank, although not beyond the realm of the world's monetary system. I might not know about all of my benefactor's accounts, and I might not know how the money got into my account. All that matters to my bank and me is that the money I withdraw does not break the laws governing the bank.

What Kind of Miracle?

Writer Tim Stafford tells a story of a young man who expected to spend the rest of his life in a wheelchair. Years of multiple surgeries had done nothing for him, and one of the top specialists in the country had told him to stop hoping for a cure and accept his excruciating pain. Then, at the invitation of a friend, he rolled his wheelchair into a church one Sunday morning. Someone prayed for him, and he walked out pain-free. Four years later, he was still without pain in his feet.

Stafford told the story to a dedicated Christian doctor, who takes the Bible at face value when it describes miracles. In this case, the doctor was skeptical. He saw many sick people, and he sometimes saw healing that was hard to predict and explain. Some people got worse unexpectedly, and others got better. The doctor did not deny the possibility of a miracle, but he observed that people sometimes heal in surprising ways, and the link between mind and body is amazingly strong.

Was the healing of the young man a miracle? If it was a miracle, did God supernaturally manipulate a nerve or bone to heal him? Would it be less of a miracle if God activated an unknown mind-body connection? If the healing happened through a mind-body connection, would the miracle be greater if the connection were energized through a *back door* to the programming of his nervous system, rather than by the young man's faith or state of mind? All could be miracles, and all could inspire a kind of awe. The greatest wonder might be how his nervous system, with healing capabilities, developed from a single cell at conception.

If God can operate across the spectrum of heaven and earth, a miracle can be defined as an unexplained mystery of God acting in accordance with his plan and purpose, while upholding the laws he ordained.

FREE WILL AND DIVINE PROVIDENCE

> The deeply-rooted belief in psychic freedom and choice is quite unscientific, and must give ground before the claims of a determinism which governs mental life.[7]
>
> —SIGMUND FREUD

I am planning to fix stir-fry tonight for dinner. I plan to do so because there is leftover chicken in the refrigerator, and my wife bought snow peas this week. On the other hand, I could decide to grill hamburgers. My choice.

Except, maybe it is not my choice. My selection might be influenced by the facts that my mother never cooked stir-fry, my father was a bargain hunter, or Costco sells rotisserie chicken at a ridiculously low price. It is constrained by my environment; in different times or places hamburger and stir-fry would not appear together on a mental menu. It might be subtly shaped by external forces: advertising, social interactions, or the smell of my neighbor's charcoal grill.

In fact, my selection will be influenced by an incredibly complex web of events, spanning the history and geography of the earth and encompassing the realms of sociology, psychology, anthropology, and economics.

If I choose to grill hamburgers, is it a personal choice, or is it an inevitable result of the history of the universe and my own personal history?

---

7. Quoted by Miriam Adeney in HIS Magazine, October 1976, 11.

Is Free Will an Illusion?

> ... the molecular basis of biology shows that biological processes are governed by the laws of physics and chemistry and therefore are as determined as the orbits of the planets. Recent experiments in neuroscience support the view that it is our physical brain, following the known laws of science, that determines our actions, and not some agency that exists outside those laws ... so it seems that we are no more than biological machines and that free will is just an illusion.[8]
>
> —Stephen Hawking and Leonard Mlodinow

Any decision—whether to eat, speak, or act in a certain way—occurs in the brain. Much of what happens in the brain is beyond conscious control or influence. It involves biology and chemistry, evolutionary development, and cultural patterns.

Choices depend upon memories and processing in the brain, which has cells and neurons, molecules and atoms, and at a more foundational level, quantum interactions. All of those can ultimately be traced back to the Big Bang. Hawking and Mlodinow argue that, if every event in the universe developed in a deterministic way from the initial state of the Big Bang, free will is an illusion.

If free will is an illusion, the thoughts in your mind right now are a product of the history of the universe; you have no choice about how you think and feel. As you read this, you have no choice about what you will do an hour from now, since that choice will inevitably flow from the current state of your brain, and ultimately, the history of the universe leading up to this point in time. Also, if you think you have a choice whether to believe God is involved in the universe, you are mistaken, for your beliefs are determined by the initial state of the universe.

Of course, if that is true, Hawking and Mlodinow do not have free will either, and they really had no choice about whether to say that free will is an illusion. Also, we have no choice about whether we believe them or not.

I am inclined to believe that I really do have choices! On the other hand, I have to admit my belief resides in my brain, and the laws of nature

---

8. Yet Hawking and Mlodinow say, "since we cannot solve the equations that determine our behavior, we use the effective theory that people have free will." (*Grand Design*, 32–33).

operate when I make a choice and act on it. How can I believe that I have free will?

Real Freedom to Choose

> This day I call the heavens and the earth as witnesses against you that I have set before you life and death, blessings and curses. Now choose life, so that you and your children may live and that you may love the Lord your God, listen to his voice, and hold fast to him. For the Lord is your life...
>
> —Deuteronomy 30:19–20

The people of Israel were slaves in Egypt. As slaves, they neglected God, forgot that God had a special purpose for them, and did not know how to love and obey God or live in a way that would create a healthy community. Then God stepped in. He led them out of Egypt, provided for their needs, and gave them laws to help them live in freedom and form a healthy community. God arranged for those things to happen.

Now the people are ready to enter the Promised Land, and they can choose their way of life. They did not have many choices in Egypt, but now they can choose, either to live in relationship to God, or to ignore him and live as they please. Their choice did not arise by chance; God made it possible.

Free will can exist only if God, who can solve the equations involving all the variables, sets up situations that allow for choices. Being personal, he can choose and act to allow for human choices. Being infinite, he can solve the equations that provide for freedom of choice within the indeterminacy of the laws of nature, thereby not undermining them.

Providence and God's Provision for Free Will

Earlier, I told a story of a young man who was healed after people prayed for him. People made choices that day. The young man chose to go to the church, as did the people who were there with him. The leaders chose to have a time of prayer, and people chose to pray. The young man chose to believe, and he rose to his feet, not only at the time of prayer, but every day after that. There were opportunities for choices, and people made good choices.

Infinitely Personal

On the other hand, it is not hard to see that God provided opportunities for those choices. The church would not have been meeting if Jesus had not come to earth. Each person in the church that day had a personal history, and the right people came together at the right time, with the right leadership and motivation to pray. It is not unreasonable to believe God was somehow involved when the young man rose to his feet.

In classical theology, the *providence* of God means that God is continually involved in the affairs of the universe, to fulfill his plan and purpose. God's *providence* includes his *provision* for the laws of nature to be upheld, as well as his loving *provision* for the needs of those he loves.[9]

God's providence does not eliminate free will or human agency. In fact, the *providence* of God *provides* for human agency, allowing people to make choices for good or evil. God *provides* opportunities for people to act in ways that are not fully determined by the history of the universe, their own personal histories, or current events.

The providence of God frees people to rise about their natural condition. Failures or insecurities of the past do not necessarily determine outcomes in the future. Feelings of rage do not inevitably control words that are spoken. Husbands and wives are not doomed to repeat the patterns that have been set early in their marriage.

In his loving providence, God provides alternate histories for those who choose to be guided by them. His love overcomes insecurity. His forgiveness erases guilt. His values overcome prejudice, his justice guides human justice, and his grace engenders gratitude. Those who see reality through God's eyes are transformed by his vision for humanity and invigorated by hope.

Providential Choices

The mail was late yesterday. Finally, in late afternoon, I left my office in the deep recesses of the church, to check the mail one more time and warm up a final few sips of coffee in the microwave. As I set my coffee cup on the counter, a friend walked through the door. We had not said much more than "Hello" for several months, but I knew he was dealing with a situation we should talk about, and I was hoping he would open up to me. Well, there he was, right in front of me, and I had a choice to make. I asked him how he was doing. He said he had not been planning to talk to me about

9. Eph 1:4–14, Heb 1:3, Jer 5:24, Acts 14:15–17.

his problem, and he appreciated that I cared. Our conversation happened because we arrived in the hallway at the same time, and because I took the opportunity to reach out to him.

Did God arrange for our meeting in the hallway, or was it only a coincidence? I don't know! I cannot begin to comprehend all of the variables that might have brought us together, and I have no idea how God would solve the equations so we would arrive at the same time and place. I feel that God made space in our unexpected meeting for me to open the conversation, and I think God prepared me, through my past growth experiences, to have the courage and motivation to speak directly and wisely. God did not script my words, but I think God providentially gave me the opportunity to say them. What do you think? Was our meeting a cosmic accident, with our words determined by our personal histories and the history of the entire universe, or was God at work to allow us the freedom of that conversation?

With Us

> Gagarin flew into space, but didn't see any god there.[1]
>
> —RUSSIAN PREMIER NIKITA KHRUSHCHEV, AFTER THE FIRST MANNED SPACEFLIGHT BY YURI GAGARIN

BEFORE HUMANS EXPLORED SPACE, it was easier to imagine that God might be found somewhere beyond the earth's atmosphere. Khrushchev was engaged in an anti-religion campaign, and he seized an opportunity to debunk such uninformed faith.

Few people today think God lives above the clouds or out in space. They are more likely to think that, if God exists, scientists should be able to find him by exploring the universe and plumbing the depths of its mysteries. Yet modern scientific methods encounter some of the same limitations as ancient attempts at finding God.

God as Designer of the Universe

> The heavens declare the glory of God; the skies
> proclaim the work of his hands.
>
> —PSALM 19:1

---

1. Wikiquote.org disputes the claim that Gagarin said, "I looked and looked and looked but I didn't see God." Gagarin was a baptized Orthodox Christian, who showed interest in the faith later in his life.

Ancient people gazed in wonder at the stars in the sky. People looking into the sky today have even more reasons to be amazed, as they understand that the universe extends for billions of light years, with countless galaxies of unimaginable size.

Some astronauts have said that seeing the earth from space is a kind of religious experience. The exquisite beauty and stunning grandeur of the universe point to a wise and ingenious designer.

Yet the designer might seem inaccessible. If we look at a beautiful building, we learn a great deal about the architect and builder. We might say that the architect is creative and brilliant, but we do not really *know* him.

God as First Cause

I live in a house that is over a hundred years old. I do not know who built it, but I am quite sure somebody did! Many people feel the same way about the universe: Somebody must have made it. This is the basis for a common argument for the existence of God: God as First Cause.

Some physicists theorize that the universe could have come into existence without a god to "light the match." Stephen Hawking said, "Because there is a law like gravity, the universe can and will create itself."[2] Lawrence Krauss speculates that the universe bubbled up from a primordial quantum vacuum. Both assume the existence of nature and its laws outside of the universe, without answering the question, "How did gravity and quantum vacuums come into existence?"[3]

The possibility of a first cause cannot be eliminated on scientific grounds, but the first cause could be almost any deity, power, or intelligence. It is like finding a stream of clear, refreshing water; it must come from somewhere, but the source could be a glacier, a spring, or a purification plant.

---

2. Hawking and Mlodinov, *Grand Design*, 180.

3. Gleiser, "Origin of the Universe." He adds, "This quantum vacuum is a very loaded nothing: It assumes the whole machinery of quantum field theory, the modern description of how elementary particles of matter interact with one another, was already in operation."

God of the Gaps

> There are reverent minds who ceaselessly scan the fields of
> Nature and the books of Science in search of gaps—gaps
> which they will fill up with God. As if God lived in gaps? . . .
> Nature is God's writing, and can only tell the truth.[4]
>
> —HENRY DRUMMOND, 1896

Throughout history, people have seen the hand of God in things they could not explain. Then, when science was able to explain what they had attributed to God, the gaps got smaller and there was less need for God.

The God of the Bible is not a god of the gaps, but the God of everything! He is the God of DNA and evolutionary adaptation, as well as the God of quarks and quantum vacuum states. Belief that God is involved in the entire universe can inspire exploration of the universe, as each discovery shows a little more about the wisdom and power of God.

Gaps in human understanding might open the door to seeking God, but they do not reveal anything about him.

God of Mystical Experience

Many people say they have had mystical or spiritual experiences at some time in their lives. Others yearn for a supernatural encounter with God.

Using PET and fMRI brain scans, scientists have determined that mystical or spiritual experiences activate specific parts of the brain, and some people are more inclined toward them than others. The fact that mystical experiences engage the brain does not necessarily make them invalid, for awareness has to happen somewhere.

Mystical experiences are common in many religions and cultures, and they vary significantly. Some people say that they hear or sense God speaking, while others describe unfocused emotional or transcendent sensations. Some lose all sense of self, and others experience heightened sensitivity to stimuli.

Mystical experiences might point to a spiritual reality beyond the physical world, but they are not dependable pathways to finding God.

---

4. Drummond, *Ascent of Man*, 426.

God through Cosmic Lenses

God of Universal Ideals

Truth. Beauty. Harmony. Love. Almost all cultures and civilizations cherish ideals like these and deny ideals like deceit, disharmony, or hatred. Betraying a friend or destroying a beautiful object for no reason seems wrong, while seeking truth or loving someone for unselfish reasons strikes a chord of idealism.

Evolutionary processes might contribute to the development of ideals like harmony and love, but it is hard to see how valuing beauty in inanimate objects would promote survival or dominance. Ideals like unselfish love and inconvenient truth point to a deeper fount of values—perhaps a noble Life-Force working in the universe.

A god of universal ideals is little more than an idea or image of goodness. Finding a god like that would be like seeking a wife from an online description. The description might use words like beautiful, caring, sensitive, intelligent, and strong. All true (or not!), but lacking substance. Who is she, really, and how does she breathe life into those adjectives?

God in the Abstract

Belief in a higher power provides a foundation for recovery from addiction, a positive outlook on life, morality, and justice. Yet vague and unfocused concepts do not connect people with God.

The Big Bang Theory was a popular television comedy, featuring brilliant scientists totally lacking in social skills. On the show, physicist Sheldon Cooper is the ultimate parody of a nerdy scientist: he believes he knows everything, and he trusts only what he can empirically verify.

Sheldon has a wealth of information about women, a flowchart on how friendships develop, and relationship contracts with his roommate and friends. One day, an unexplainable sensation engulfs him, and he wonders whether a parasite has invaded his brain. He recognizes that the sensation arises from his relationship with his friend, Amy. His abstract ideas of love were empty until Amy brought them into focus.

Nature, intuition, and logic provide hints of God, but how can God be truly *known*?

With Us

GENERAL AND PARTICULAR KNOWLEDGE

> Scientists love generality, and they are often wary of particularity. Professionally we are concerned with the laws of nature, which are believed to be the same at all times and places . . . Ideas of a multiverse seem to have become popular because they represent a way of swallowing up this embarrassing cosmic particularity in wider generality of a proliferation of different worlds.[5]
>
> —John Polkinghorne

Science depends upon the *generality* of the laws of nature. For example, gravity applies on the surface of the earth or the moon, at the atomic level, and in the far reaches of the universe.

Generalized laws of nature emerge from repeatable experiments or observations. A ball can be dropped ten times, with the same result each time. The earth circles the sun every day, with the same schedule year after year.

Yet human life does not always conform to generalities. The sun rises on unique individuals, each with their own perspective on the dawning of a new day. It shines on battlefields littered with bodies, as well as on children playing in their yards. It struggles to penetrate a cloud of nuclear winter, or it shines on a wedding on the beach.

The Particularity of Human Experience

> We understand each other's dark souls so well, and also drinking coffee and eating sausages, etc.[6]
>
> —Albert Einstein, letter to Mileva Maric

Scientists employ *generality* in their work, but love is with a *particular* person in a *particular* way. Einstein's relationship with Mileva Maric developed in *particular* times of drinking coffee and eating sausages, while plumbing the depths of their *particular* personalities.

In his scientific work, Einstein developed general principles and laws, such as the photoelectric effect and relativity. At the same time, he engaged with the peculiarities of other scientists and the tumultuous political

---

5. Polkinghorne, *Science and the Trinity*, 170–71.
6. Isaacson, *Einstein*, 33.

movements of his time, which are not amenable to repetition, theoretical analysis, or generalized principles of behavior.

The Particularity of History

History is mostly concerned with *particularity*. Historians might compare the Roman Caesars to rulers throughout history, but there was only one Julius Caesar, one Augustus Caesar, and one Nero, and each one left a unique mark on history.

History does not allow for repetition. There was one Battle of Waterloo, and there is no way to go back in time to observe it personally. The battle cannot be repeated, since world conditions and human characteristics will never be the same, and Napoleon is no longer alive.

Historical observations are not verifiable by repetition, but they can be evaluated for consistency with contemporaneous observations and outcomes from the event. Thus, accounts of the Battle of Waterloo are considered to be valid if they are consistent with primary sources from the time period, the flow of history after the battle, and the fact that France does not rule the world today.

God Revealed in Human History

Theologians describe God in *generality*: God is powerful, all-knowing, omnipresent, gracious, and just. Yet those concepts stem from *particular* words and actions. Events in the Old Testament demonstrate God's power, faithfulness, mercy, and patience. His words express his concern for righteousness, social justice, and faithful human relationships. Personal encounters reveal how he interacts with people, and inspired words give insight into his eternal plan and purpose.

Biblical events cannot be repeated, but they support a unified picture of a God that engages in human history, is faithful to his promises, and desires a relationship with people.

The Particularity of Jesus Christ

> The Word [Greek *logos*] became flesh and made his dwelling among us. We have seen his glory, the glory of the one and only Son, who

> came from the Father, full of grace and truth ... No one has ever seen God, but the one and only Son, who is himself God and is in closest relationship with the Father, has made him known.
>
> —JOHN 1:14, 18

In the secular Greek world, *logos* had been adopted as a technical term in developing sciences, such as grammar, logic, rhetoric, psychology and metaphysics, theology, and mathematics. Jews in that culture understood the *logos* of God as an expression of God himself, for God's words revealed his will and carried his power and authority. Thus John 1:1 says, ". . . the Word was God."

The *logos* of God came to earth, not as a book of wisdom, a description of God's attributes, or a philosophical treatise, but in the body of a particular man. The glory of God—his grace and truth—was revealed in the historical life of Jesus of Nazareth. How could this be?

JESUS: THE PARADOX OF THE GOD-MAN

> I and the Father are one.
>
> —JOHN 10:30

Who was Jesus? He was a man, one of many humans to walk on the earth. He was sometimes tired, hungry, and thirsty. He experienced a full range of human emotions, from joy to sorrow, compassion to anger. He died, and his body was laid in a tomb.

Yet the New Testament writers assert that Jesus was unique among humanity. He claimed to be God, and he demonstrated the power of God by healing people and controlling the forces of nature. His followers were finally convinced of his deity when he rose from the dead, and at the beginning of the Christian movement, Peter confidently declared that the man who was crucified and raised from the dead was "both Lord and Christ."[7]

The apostle Paul, writing in the early days of the church, spoke of "the human ancestry of Christ, who is God over all" (Rom 9:5). The author of Hebrews identified Jesus as "the radiance of God's glory and the exact

---

7. Acts 2:32–39. Peter's words implied that Jesus was God, since *Lord* was the Old Testament referent to Yahweh. In addition, Peter said that Jesus was raised from the dead, offers forgiveness of sins, and sends the Holy Spirit.

representation of his being, sustaining all things by his powerful word" (Heb 1:3).

The claims of Jesus and the church challenge the limitations of logic and experience, and believers struggle to wrap their minds around the paradox of Jesus as fully human and fully divine.

Defining the Paradox

In the early centuries after Jesus, theologians tried to eliminate the paradox of Jesus as both God and man. Some denied that Jesus was God, and others denied that the Son of God was actually a man. The paradox could not be eliminated, because the New Testament supports both the humanity and the divinity of Jesus.

In the fourth and fifth centuries, church councils were convened to resolve the paradox, or at least to define the boundaries of orthodoxy.[8] The Council of Chalcedon in AD 451 was the most definitive, declaring the Lord Jesus Christ to be of the same being or essence (Greek *homoousios*) with both God and humanity—one person in two natures. The definition did little to resolve the paradox; it merely restated it in a clearer and more forceful way.

Efforts to resolve the paradox of Jesus as God and man were similar in some respects to efforts of physicists to describe an electron without reference to the mysteries of quantum theory. Is an electron a particle? Yes, but not in the same way that a speck of dust is a particle. Is it a wave? Yes, but not like a wave of water. Paradox points to deeper reality.

A MYSTERY OF DYNAMIC MOVEMENT

The paradox of Jesus as both God and man cannot be resolved by careful definitions and distinctions. It is a mystery, not to be solved, but to be celebrated.

One way to view the mystery is in terms of *dynamic movements*: God taking human form, and a man being filled with God. Those movements are captured in two New Testament Greek words: *kenosis* and *pleroma*.[9]

---

8. Pelikan, *Emergence of the Catholic Tradition*, 226–77.

9. Hunter, *Jesus, Lord and Saviour*, 115–17. Hunter puts a different slant on both ideas, especially *plerosis*.

Kenosis: The Son of God Limited Himself

> [Christ Jesus], though he was in the form of God, did not count equality with God a thing to be grasped, but emptied himself, by taking the form of a servant, being born in the likeness of men.
>
> —Philippians 2:6–7, ESV

The Greek verb *kenao* means *empty* or *render useless*. Taking the form of a man, the Son of God shed some of his attributes. In particular, he accepted limitations of three divine characteristics: glory, privileges, and powers unique to God.

Limitations on Glory

> Nazareth! Can anything good come from there? Nathanael asked. "Come and see," said Philip.
>
> —John 1:46

> "I have brought you glory on earth by finishing the work you gave me to do. And now, Father, glorify me in your presence with the glory I had with you before the world began."
>
> —John 17:4–5

The glory of God in heaven is hard to imagine. When Moses spent time in the presence of God, his face shone. When Isaiah had a vision, he fell to the ground, saying, "Woe to me. I am ruined." In the Apostle John's vision of Christ ascended into heaven, ten thousand times ten thousand angels, along with every creature in heaven and earth, proclaim the worth of the Lamb who redeemed all creation.[10]

The Son laid aside some of his heavenly glory when he came to earth. Contrary to medieval art, there was not a halo above the head of the baby Jesus. His parents were common people, from a small village in a backward area of a small country. As if to emphasize his lack of glory, Jesus was born (it was said) as an illegitimate child.

---

10. Exod 34:29–35, Isa 6:5, Rev 5:1–13.

God through Cosmic Lenses

Limitations on Privileges

> As they were walking along the road, a man said to Jesus, "I will follow you wherever you go." Jesus replied, "Foxes have dens and birds have nests, but the Son of Man has no place to lay his head."
>
> —LUKE 9:57–58

It is hard to imagine that the Creator of the universe might ever lack anything he needs or wants. Yet Jesus went without food in the wilderness for forty days. He depended upon wealthy women to support him. He asked a Samaritan woman to help him get a drink of water from a well. He cried out from the cross, "I am thirsty."

Jesus did not live a life of privilege. He could have chosen to be a carpenter or a respected rabbi with a wife and children and all the benefits of political connections. Instead, he chose a life of poverty and persecution, owning only one set of clothing at his death.

Limitations on Power

> The hands that had made the sun and stars were too small to reach the huge heads of the cattle.[11]
>
> —G.K. CHESTERTON

God has unique powers, which he does not share with humans. Some words used to describe them are based on the Latin root *omni* (all-): God is *omnipotent* (all-powerful), *omniscient* (all-knowing), and *omnipresent* (everywhere-present).

For God the Son to be truly human, he had to lay aside or limit those powers. The baby Jesus was not omnipotent; he was not able to feed himself. The man Jesus was not omniscient; he did not know calculus, and he did not know the time of his return. Jesus was not omnipresent; he could not simultaneously be in both Palestine and China.

The Son of God became a man by limiting his divine glory, privileges, and power. That downward movement was accompanied by an upward movement: The man, Jesus, became God as he was filled with glory, privileges, and power.

11. As quoted in Yancey, "Paradox of Great Price," 29.

Pleroma: God Filled Jesus

> For God was pleased to have all his fullness [Gk., *pleroma*] dwell in him ... For in Christ all the fullness of the Deity lives in bodily form.
>
> —COLOSSIANS 1:19, 2:9

Can a glass be full of water? Of course, but can it contain the fullness of water? That is a deeper question! The fullness of water encompasses the waves of the ocean, the roar of Niagara Falls, the dew on the grass, and an essential element in every human cell. Water is relief for the thirsty, as well as a grave for the drowning. Can a glass contain all of that? Not really, although it can contain a full measure of water—true water, fully water, as full as a glass can hold.

When the apostle Paul says the fullness of God lived in the body of Jesus, he is speaking of a mystery. He is not saying that all of the attributes of God were expressed in the body of Jesus—at least, not in all the ways that they can be expressed in all of God's Reality. He is saying, quite remarkably, that every bit of Jesus was full of God.

Full of God's Glory

> For God ... made his light shine in our hearts to give us the light
> of the knowledge of God's glory displayed in the face of Christ.
>
> —2 CORINTHIANS 4:6

There was something glorious about Jesus. His miracles. His teaching. The way he treated people. His compassion. His strength. His confidence. His deep understanding and wisdom. His love.

The glory of God shone in everything Jesus did.

Full of God's Privileges

> [Jesus] was even calling God his own Father, making himself
> equal with God ... [Jesus said], "the Son can do nothing by
> himself; he can do only what he sees his Father doing, because
> whatever the Father does the Son also does. For the Father loves

> the Son and shows him all he does ... For just as the Father raises the dead and gives them life, even so the Son gives life to whom he is pleased to give it ... as the Father has life in himself, so he has granted the Son also to have life in himself.
>
> —JOHN 5:18–26

Individual Jews would not dare to identify God as their own *Father*. Old Testament believers could depend upon God's fatherly care, but they did not presume to have the rights and privileges of sons.

As God's Son, Jesus claimed the authority of his Father. He was more than a prophet who relayed messages from God; he spoke with the authority of his Father. He even claimed the right to give life to people who were dead spiritually or physically.

Full of God's Power

> Then Jesus got into the boat and his disciples followed him. Suddenly a furious storm came up on the lake, so that the waves swept over the boat. But Jesus was sleeping. The disciples went and woke him, saying, "Lord, save us! We're going to drown!" He replied, "You of little faith, why are you so afraid?" Then he got up and rebuked the winds and the waves, and it was completely calm. The men were amazed and asked, "What kind of man is this? Even the winds and the waves obey him!"
>
> —MATTHEW 8:23–27

The incident on the lake showed the human limitations of Jesus, as well as his divine power. As a man, he was tired, he needed sleep, and he was not aware that the storm threatened the lives of everyone in the boat. Yet, filled with the authority of God, he commanded the winds and waves to be calm, and they became calm. There were many incidents like that, where the words of Jesus carried the authority and power of God.

In terms of knowledge, Jesus did not know everything; yet he knew much about what people were thinking and doing. Jesus said that he did not know when the end would come; yet he knew a lot about the events leading up to it. As a boy of twelve, Jesus was still "growing in wisdom and knowledge"; yet he knew enough to amaze the most knowledgeable Jewish scholars. Jesus could not be more than one place at a time; yet he always seemed to know where he should be. Despite his human limitations, Jesus was full of the power of God.

Embracing the Mystery

> Beyond all question, the mystery from which true godliness springs is great: He appeared in the flesh, was vindicated by the Spirit, was seen by angels, was preached among the nations, was believed on in the world, was taken up in glory.
>
> —1 Timothy 3:16

This ancient Christian hymn celebrates a mystery beyond human comprehension: God and man together in the person of Jesus. It is not a paradox to be resolved, but a mystery to be embraced as a source of life with God.

Imagine a prince, the heir to the throne, in a kingdom of humble peasants. The prince has everything: prestige, privileges, and power. The peasants have none of that.

The prince does an amazing thing: He lays aside his royal robes, leaves the castle, and lives in a humble abode in the poorest part of his kingdom. He has laid aside his prestige. He has left behind the privileges of life in the castle: the finest of everything, servants to do his bidding, and immediate access to every resource of the king. He no longer has horses to carry him to every corner of the kingdom. He no longer sits in on the daily royal briefing, aware of all that is happening in the lands beyond. He has laid aside all of that.

Yet there is something about this humble man. He is confident, benevolent, even gracious. He speaks out of personal experience of his love for the good and righteous king. He does not approach life as a victim of circumstances, but as a master of them. He has a quiet strength and confidence, and he sees great potential in every person he meets.

In a sense, the prince is a peasant, and the peasant is a prince! By embracing him as both peasant and prince, the peasants gain new insight into the king and themselves.

The mystery of the Son of God is even greater. Not only does the Son live as a human, but humans are invited to share the life of the Son.

Life Full of Goodness

> I have come that they may have life, and have it to the full.
>
> —JOHN 10:10

In John's gospel, Jesus' first miraculous sign occurred at a wedding feast. The host had run out of wine, and Jesus changed the water in several large jars into wine. It was not cheap wine, which would be acceptable when everybody has been drinking in excess; it was the finest wine—better than the wine at the first toast.

The story is a sign of life in God's kingdom. Jesus brought life, not only to gatherings of family and friends, but also to gatherings of "tax collectors and sinners." He gave life to lepers, the deaf and the blind, prostitutes, a shady businessman, and people bored with their "pretty good" lives.

Jesus came to bring the good life of God into the world, and his followers can share the goodness of life with him.

Life as a Child of God

> When the set time had fully come, God sent his Son, born of a woman . . . that we might receive adoption to sonship. Because you are his sons, God sent the Spirit of his Son into our hearts, the Spirit who calls out, "Abba, Father." So you are no longer a slave, but God's child; and since you are his child, God has made you also an heir.
>
> —GALATIANS 4:4–7

Abba is an Aramaic word, a familiar variant of the Aramaic word for father, *ab*. The word is written without translation in the text, because it was characteristically used by Jesus.

Paul says that those who belong to Christ and have his Spirit in their hearts are children of God. Although Jesus is the *only-begotten* Son of God (John 3:16), believers "receive adoption to sonship;" they are part of God's family.

Two of my grandchildren are adopted. They are confident in their identity in the family, and they enjoy the benefits of belonging. They share family resources, accept family responsibilities, and will share in any family inheritance.

With Us

God invites people to be adopted as his children. His children are confident in their relationship with him, they share in the responsibilities and benefits of his family, and they have an eternal inheritance.

Life of Extraordinary Potential

> Whoever believes in me will do the works I have been doing, and they will do even greater things than these, because I am going to the Father.
>
> —JOHN 14:12

What are the limits of human potential? Modern technology is quite advanced, but it does not compare to the power of Jesus to calm a raging sea, using nothing more than his voice. Medical science brings amazing healing, but Jesus healed with a word and a touch. Human wisdom continues to advance, but the teaching of Jesus amazed people with the depth of God's wisdom.

Was Jesus able to do those things because he was God? He *was* God—but the amazing part was that he did those things as a man, full of God. If he could do those things as a man, what are the limits of human potential?

As I was writing this chapter, I read of the death of Jerry Bridges. Jerry was born during the Great Depression, to parents who were cotton farmers in Texas. He was cross-eyed, deaf in one ear, and he had spine and breastbone deformities, which were not corrected because his family could not afford the cost of medical care. He was able to attend college by enlisting in the Navy, but he was discharged because of his eyesight within two years.

Jerry began working with a Christian organization, The Navigators, and he worked first as an administrative assistant and then as Secretary-Treasurer. Never flashy, he labored behind the scenes for decades. He began writing a book when he was nearly fifty years old, and *The Pursuit of Holiness*, based on his own spiritual journey, sold 1.5 million copies. He went on to write more than twenty books.

No one fulfills their human potential to the degree that Jesus did. Yet Jesus demonstrates the extraordinary potential available in a relationship with the Father.

A NEW WAY OF BEING HUMAN

> The Son of God became a man to enable
> men to become sons of God.[12]
>
> —C.S. Lewis

> In Christ all the fullness [Greek *pleroma*] of the Deity lives in bodily form, and you have been given fullness [*pleroma*] in Christ.
>
> —Colossians 2:9–10

This is remarkable! The *pleroma* of the deity is in Christ, and the Apostle Paul says that believers are also given *pleroma* in Christ!

To what degree can people be like Christ? There are obvious human limitations, and neither Lewis nor Paul meant to say that humans can become gods. Yet there seems to be no limit to how full of God people can be, except for their own capacity to be filled.

What limits human capacity for God's fullness? Think of a spring of water, and a jug being filled from the spring. To be filled, the opening must be large enough, the jug must be free of dirt and contaminants, and any cracks or holes must be repaired, so that water will not leak out.

Being filled with God is a lifelong process. It begins as faith creates openness to God. It continues as sin is rooted out through repentance, and the water of life takes its place. It involves a lifetime of repair and restoration of a cracked and broken life.

The process begins with openness to the possibility of God making people more like Jesus.

---

12. Lewis, *Mere Christianity*, 139.

For Us

> The creation was subjected to frustration ... in hope that
> the creation itself will be liberated from its bondage to decay
> and brought into the freedom and glory of the children of
> God ... In all things God works for the good of those who love
> him, who have been called according to his purpose ...
>
> —ROMANS 8:20, 28

IT IS SPRING, AND I am sitting in a wooden rocker on my expansive front porch. There has been a lot of rain this year, and the grass is a deep green, the flowers are in bloom, and the trees stand out in shades of green and plum against the clear blue sky. I hear at least seven different kinds of birds chirping and calling to each other. Did God make such a wonderful world for people like me?

Last week, I wandered beneath one of those same trees, and one of those chirping birds pooped on my shirt! The week before, one of the thunderstorms that made the grass so green dropped softball-sized hail, which crashed through the roofs of houses. The roofers finished re-shingling our roof yesterday, but now we have no TV dish. It will take two weeks to get someone to come and realign the dish! Is God behind that too?

I feel ashamed to focus on my small problems, when millions of people are homeless, oppressed by cruel governments, or victims of natural or environmental disasters. Some have birth defects or diseases carried by mosquitoes. Why are there mosquitoes?

God through Cosmic Lenses

Humanity inhabits a world of beauty and wonder, as well as ugliness and frustration. Is that a cosmic accident, or does God have a purpose for placing humanity in a world like this?

A FINE-TUNED UNIVERSE

> If almost any of the basic features of the universe, from the properties of atoms to the distribution of the galaxies, were different, life would very probably be impossible.[1]
>
> —Paul Davies

Why is the universe as it is? Is the design of the universe haphazard, like paint flung against a wall until beauty and function appear? Or is the design as intricately structured as a fine racing car or a classical symphony?

A fruitful universe—one that produces carbon-based life—must take a rather particular form. Many features of the universe must be "fine-tuned" for human life to exist.[2]

- *Fundamental forces of nature.* John Polkinghorne identifies four fundamental forces that correspond to four constant values: "The fine structure constant (α) specifies the strength of electromagnetism. Newton's gravitational constant (G) specifies the strength of gravity; and two constants specify the strengths of the nuclear forces, g_s for the strong forces that hold the nucleus together, and g_w for the weak forces that cause some nuclear decays and also control the interactions of neutrinos. The magnitudes of all these constants are tightly constrained if the universe is to be capable of producing life."

- *Carbon energy resonance.* Resonance at a particular energy in carbon allowed carbon to persist over oxygen in stars, causing Fred Hoyle, an atheist who identified the resonance, to say that the universe appeared to be "a put-up job."

- *The value of the cosmological constant (λ).* The cosmological constant is associated with a kind of antigravity, driving matter apart. The constant is remarkably smaller than particle physics would predict; in fact, it is smaller by 120 orders of magnitude (10^{-120}). Steven Weinberg

1. Davies, *Cosmic Jackpot*, 2.
2 Polkinghorne, "Anthropic Principle."

observed that if it were only 10^{-119} smaller than predicted, the universe would have expanded too rapidly to form stars.

- *Initial Conditions.* When the universe was around 10^{-43} seconds old, initial velocities and gravitational forces had to be in a narrowly defined range, to allow for the right kind of expansion. A difference of one part in 10^{60} would have made a universe like ours impossible. In addition, Roger Penrose emphasized the need for extremely low entropy, with odds of that happening by chance to be one in ten to the power of 10^{123}.

- *Size of the Universe.* The universe might seem unnecessarily large for life on earth to exist. However, only a universe as big as ours could have lasted the almost fourteen billion years required to produce the elements needed for life, as well as small, rocky planets such as earth. If the universe were significantly smaller, stars such as the sun would start to burn out before human life formed, and stable planetary systems would be impossible.

- *Open Character.* There must be enough order in the universe to allow the laws of nature to hold. However, there must be enough openness to chance (or God!) for true novelty. In other words, quantum uncertainty is necessary for a universe! If the universe developed according to Newtonian determinism, there would be no stars or planets, nor supernovae to form heavier metals. However, if the universe developed haphazardly, nothing new would persist, and neither the orbit of the earth nor cell reproduction would be possible.

The Anthropic Principle

> The more I examine the universe, and the details of its
> architecture, the more evidence I find that the Universe
> in some sense must have known we were coming.[3]
>
> —Freeman Dyson

The idea that the universe is fine-tuned for life is widely accepted, although the source and purpose of the fine-tuning is vigorously debated.

---

3. Dyson, *Disturbing the Universe*, 318.

The *Weak Anthropic Principle* (WAP) states the obvious: If the universe were not "just right" for human life, humans would not be observing it. The conclusion seems trivial, but it does generate a kind of wonder at the degree of fine-tuning required for humanity to exist.

The *Strong Anthropic Principle* (SAP) is more contentious, for it says that the universe *had to have* properties that would allow for the development of human life. As John Polkinghorne puts it, "The universe was billions of years old before life appeared in it, but it was pregnant with life from the beginning."[4]

The Anthropic Principle, whether in strong or weak forms, leaves open questions of "Why?" or "How?" so many conditions of the universe are compatible with human life.

Who or What Is Behind It All?

If I opened my front door and found a million dollars in a box with my name on it, how would I explain it? Would I think it was just my lucky day? Would I assume that someone arranged for me to receive the money? Would I assume that I must have done something to cause the money to appear in a box with my name on it?

If the universe emerged with humanity's name on it, how did that happen? Theories fall into four categories:

Chance

Multiverse theories assume that there are a very large number of universes, each with different laws of nature and different parameters. With so many universes, one of those universes might be structured "just right" to produce carbon-based, sentient life. That lucky universe would be ours, of course, since we are here to observe it.

Multiverse theories do not necessarily exclude the involvement of a deity or intelligence in the multiverse and our universe in particular. However, attributing the structure of the universe and the emergence of human life to chance *alone* reduces humanity to a fortunate cosmic accident.

---

4. Polkinghorne, "Anthropic Principle."

For Us

Humanity

The *Participatory Anthropic Principle* (PAP) speculates that, out of many potential forms of the universe, human observers determine the particular form of the universe in which the observers exist. In this view, humanity has a role in determining the laws of nature, from the beginning of time and space into its future.[5]

Human participation in the future of the universe is not so hard to accept. Humans are able to advance the cause of knowledge and manipulate the universe through technology. They create artificial intelligence, and they dream of expanding the scope of human existence by colonizing other worlds. Some people believe they can change the world by their thoughts, or that wishing makes dreams come true.

It is harder to believe that human participation might influence the past or create the laws of nature that emerged at the earliest beginning of the universe. Proponents of PAP often appeal to a specious interpretation of quantum theory, "observer-created reality."

Cosmic Intelligence

The intricate structure of the universe causes some people to imagine a cosmic intelligence that fine-tunes the universe and governs the laws of nature. Some envision an impersonal force or guiding principle, akin to Einstein's "The Old One," while others ascribe cosmic intelligence to an elusive Grand Unified Theory (GUT) governing the formation of the universe.

God

Christians and other theists believe that God created the universe as a place for humans to live. It should be noted that this belief does not preclude the possibility that God had additional intentions for the universe, including the potential of extra-terrestrial life.[6]

---

5. Redfern, "Anthropic Principle." On the radio broadcast, PAP proponent John A. Wheeler said, "Modern quantum theory . . . leads to . . . a view that man, or intelligent life, or communicating observer participators are the whole means by which the very universe is created; without them, nothing. . . . We are participators in bringing into being not only the near and here but the far away and long ago."

6. The possibility of other worlds has a long history among Christian writers. Robert Boyle (1627–91), known for Boyle's Law of the inverse relationship between pressure

God through Cosmic Lenses

The universe God created displays his glory and goodness, and it is a beautiful, awe-inspiring environment, in which humans thrive. At the same time, some characteristics of life on earth are hard to reconcile with the goodness of God. If the universe is fine-tuned for human life, it sometimes seems to be out of tune.

Discordant Notes

> My life has been remarkably happy, perhaps in the upper 99.99 percentile of human happiness, but even so, I have seen a mother die painfully of cancer, a father's personality destroyed by Alzheimer's disease, and scores of second and third cousins murdered in the Holocaust. Signs of a benevolent designer are pretty well hidden.[7]
>
> —Steven Weinberg

Earthquakes. Tsunamis. Tornadoes. Wildfires. Plagues. Not to mention human-caused disasters like genocide, human trafficking, and ecological destruction. Those things seem out of place in a fine-tuned universe.

If the universe is solely a product of *Chance*, discord in the universe is unsurprising. Fine-tuning extends to factors critical for human life, but it might not extend to factors not as critical. Suffering and death are not ideal, but they do make sense, since they can co-exist with a fruitful universe. The only thing that does not make sense is the instinctive human feeling that the world should not have so much suffering. Where does that feeling come from?

If *Humanity* shapes the universe, discord in the universe is harder to explain. Since humanity would not knowingly choose a history contrary to its own self-interest, the discord in the universe might be traced to disorder or conflict within humanity itself.

---

and volume in a gas, wrote, "Now if we grant with some modern Philosophers, that God has made other Worlds besides this of ours, it will be highly probable that he has there display'd His manifold Wisedom, in productions very differing from those wherein we here admire it." (Boyle, "High Veneration," 172). C.S. Lewis raised the possibility of other life forms in the universe, and his science fiction trilogy imagined other life forms with a purpose and relationship to God different from humans.

7. Weinberg, "Designer Universe?"

For Us

If an amoral *Impersonal Intelligence* shapes the universe, discord is neither good nor bad. The universe is as it is, and human judgments about how the universe should be are baseless.

If a good and powerful *God* created a universe fine-tuned for human existence, the purpose of discord in the universe is a mystery. Why would God create a universe fine-tuned for life, and yet allow so much discord and distress in it?

An Evolutionary Necessity?

> The engine that has driven the three to four billion year history of terrestrial life has been the genetic mutation of germ cells, producing new possibilities for life and turning a world that originally had contained only single-celled organisms into a world that is now the home of self-conscious beings. Yet if germ cells are to mutate in this way, it is inevitable that somatic cells will also sometimes mutate and become malignant. You cannot have one without the other. Fruitful process entangles order and disorder in an inextricable way. The presence of cancer in creation, anguishing a fact through it is, is not something gratuitous that a Creator who was more competent or more compassionate could readily have eliminated.[8]
>
> —John Polkinghorne

Polkinghorne points out that evolutionary processes are by nature full of "blind alleys and ragged edges." The biological processes that allow for evolutionary progress also produce cancer, causing pain, sorrow, and death.

God could have created human life without utilizing evolutionary processes. He could have created a static universe rather than a developing one, and he could have preserved humans in a protected environment, as in the Garden of Eden. In God's wisdom, however, a discordant universe is suitable for human growth.

---

8. Polkinghorne, "Scripture and an Evolving Creation," 169.

Death: The Price of Progress?

> No one wants to die. Even people who want to go to heaven don't want to die to get there. And yet death is the destination we all share. No one has ever escaped it. And that is as it should be, because death is very likely the single best invention of life. It is life's change agent. It clears out the old to make way for the new. Right now the new is you, but someday not too long from now, you will gradually become the old and be cleared away. Sorry to be so dramatic, but it is quite true.[9]
>
> —Steve Jobs, Founder of Apple

Steve Jobs had cancer, and he died shortly after this eloquent and moving statement in a commencement address at Stanford University. Jobs found comfort in being part of the progression and renewal of human life. It might be cold comfort, however, when he is dead and gone, and his family and friends remain to mourn his passing.

If death makes way for change on a global level, it leaves behind a haunting personal question, as stated in Jas 4:14, "What is your life? You are a mist that appears for a little while and then vanishes." What is the meaning of human joy and sadness, love and pain, creativity and despair, or memories left behind?

Humanity's Role in the Universe

> Which is the real drama? Is it the evolution of the universe, with the rise of life on earth and the history of humanity a mere curiosity, a freak sideshow doomed to extinction and oblivion? Or is the story of humanity the real drama, with the vast panorama of the universe merely a background?[10]
>
> —Christopher Kaiser

Dr. Kaiser has doctoral degrees in both astrophysics and theology, giving him an appreciation of the grand development of the universe and its

---

9. "Speech at Stanford University, 2005," *The Guardian*, October 6, 2011.
10. Kaiser, "Scientist's View of the Universe," 162–71.

incomprehensible size and complexity. Yet he suggests that God created the universe as a stage for a more profound drama, with God and humanity as the key actors. What is humanity's role in the divine drama?

Dust in the Cosmos?

> We live on a hunk of rock and metal that orbits a humdrum star in the obscure outskirts of an ordinary galaxy comprised of 400 billion stars in a universe of some hundred billion galaxies . . . We have not been given the lead in the cosmic drama.[11]
>
> —CARL SAGAN

Humanity occupies a minuscule corner of the immense stage of the universe. The human drama lasts for only a few millennia, until a catastrophic event destroys life or the stars recede into obscurity. If the significance of human life depends on size or scope on a cosmic level, neither Sagan's musings nor the greatest of human endeavors are worthy of any notice at all. Human knowledge and achievements are then like dust in the cosmos.

Meaningful Dust?

> (In response to a question about whether his view of the world was not similar to that of Shakespeare's Macbeth, [Life is but] "A tale told by an idiot, filled with sound and fury, signifying nothing.") Yes, at a sort of cosmic level, it is. But what I want to guard against is people therefore getting nihilistic in their personal lives. I don't see any reason for that at all. You can have a very happy and fulfilled personal life even if you think the universe at large is a tale told by an idiot.[12]
>
> —RICHARD DAWKINS

If the actors in a play have no past or future roles, no audience, and no impact beyond the stage, will they care about their roles? Perhaps. Being happy and fulfilling one's potential are better than not being happy and

11. D'Souza, *What's So Great about God*, 32.
12. Miele, "Darwin's Dangerous Disciple."

wasting one's potential. Yet if all the action takes place in a room of no meaning, it is as if the actors are rearranging deck chairs on a sinking ship.

Playing at Life?

> All the world's a stage, And all the men and women merely players.[13]
>
> —WILLIAM SHAKESPEARE, AS YOU LIKE IT

Life is full of drama. From the first cry of a newborn to the last gasp before death, innumerable scenes celebrate life and mourn loss. People wrestle with good and evil, justice and wrong, nobleness and depravity. They experience joy and sorrow, hope and fear, pleasure and pain. They enter into collective dramas, involving science and the arts, love and war, ambitious plans and intimate encounters.

What is the meaning of those human dramas? When the play ends and the lights go out, will the actors and audience fade into oblivion? Will their struggles, passions, and achievements be forgotten, or will the impact of their drama have enduring significance?

A COSMIC DRAMA

> The awful thing is that beauty is mysterious as well as terrible. God and the devil are fighting there, and the battlefield is the heart of man.[14]
>
> —FYODOR DOSTOEVSKY, THE BROTHERS KARAMAZOV

Beyond the dramatic beauty of the universe and the drama of human history, Dostoevsky recognized a larger drama—a struggle between God and the devil. Humans have key roles on earth, but the drama extends beyond the bounds of the universe.

---

13 Shakespeare, *As You Like It*, 124.
14 Dostoevsky, *Brothers Karamazov*, 118.

For Us

Evil Powers

> Then war broke out in heaven. Michael and his angels fought against the dragon, and the dragon and his angels fought back. But he was not strong enough, and they lost their place in heaven. The great dragon was hurled down—that ancient serpent called the devil, or Satan, who leads the whole world astray. He was hurled to the earth, and his angels with him.
>
> —Revelation 12:7–9

The backstory of the earthly drama is in heaven, with heavenly beings in key roles. One of those is an Evil One, who is variously described as a dragon, Satan, the devil, Beelzebub, or the great serpent. In the apocalyptic imagery of Revelation, he and his angels fight against the archangel Michael and his angels, causing some people to identify Satan as a powerful, evil archangel.

The origin of the Evil One is unclear. If God created him, he rebelled against God, and it is likely that angels joined in his rebellion. The Bible hints of the essence of evil as hubris, leading to rebellion against God.

The Evil One is not a god, and his power is limited by God. Still, he creates mayhem on the earth: hatred, discord, suffering, pain, injustice, abuse, and death. He is an enemy of humanity, a liar who leads people astray, and their accuser when they fail to do right (Job 1:6–11; Rev 12:12).

The Evil One challenges God's power and authority. He relentlessly seeks to find fault with God, attempting to undermine God's perfect righteousness and justice. If his attacks on God were to succeed, the moral foundations of heaven and earth would crumble, and evil would prevail.

A Stage for Good and Evil

> God saw all that he had made, and it was very good.
>
> —Genesis 1:31

> Who trusted God was love indeed
> And love Creation's final law
> Tho' Nature, red in tooth and claw

With ravine, shriek'd against his creed.[15]

—ALFRED LORD TENNYSON

Genesis asserts that the world God created was "very good." Yet science indicates that the earth has always been a place of violent struggle and death. How can a world of violence and death be good?

Our friends traveled to Africa, and one of the highlights of their trip was a safari into the bush country, where they observed lions stalking a large herd of wildebeest. My friends said that a lion killing a wildebeest is a wonderful sight to behold.

Lions are made to kill and eat, and a pride of lions hunting in the wild is a beautiful thing, as Ps 104:21 celebrates: "The lions roar for their prey and seek their food from God." Yet while lions stalking their prey can be good, a mass murderer stalking and killing is not beautiful, but ugly and evil.

The world God created is good, in the sense that it is perfect for a cosmic struggle between good and evil. In a world open to both good and evil, the goodness and glory of God can be seen, while the Evil One can sow destruction. In a world like that, humans can choose between good and evil.

A Human Choice to Participate in the Battle between Good and Evil

> The LORD God said, "The man has now become like one of us, knowing good and evil. He must not be allowed to reach out his hand and take also from the tree of life and eat, and live forever." So the LORD God banished him from the Garden of Eden to work the ground from which he had been taken. After he drove the man out, he placed on the east side of the Garden of Eden cherubim and a flaming sword flashing back and forth to guard the way to the tree of life.
>
> —GENESIS 3:22–24

Genesis does not say the entire earth was a nonviolent paradise before Adam and Eve. It describes the Garden of Eden as a sheltered environment, where the trees bore perfect fruit and the animals were not dangerous to humans.

---

15. Alfred Lord Tennyson, *In Memoriam A.H.H.*, Canto 56.

For Us

God gave Adam and Eve the option of remaining in the sheltered environment of the garden, where evil was excluded. Instead, they chose to "know good and evil," and the natural consequence of their choice was expulsion into a world in which good and evil were in a constant state of conflict. The world outside the garden was open to weeds, pain, and death, and Adam and Eve got their wish: They knew good and evil.

Their choice is archetypical: They represent all of humanity, who choose to know both good and evil. Although some people might think they wouldn't choose to know evil if they had a choice, the history of humanity shows solidarity with Adam and Eve.

When Adam and Eve left the protection of the garden, the stage was set for an arduous battle between good and evil, in which there would be casualties. What would be God's role in the battle? Would he abandon the stage, leaving humanity to fight for the triumph of good over evil? Would he watch from a safe distance, avoiding the pain and distress of the struggle? Would he swoop down to make things right on the earth, or would he blow up the stage as a bad experiment?

The Plot

> Once you assume a creator and a plan, it makes humans
> objects in a cruel experiment whereby we are created
> [to be] sick and commanded to be well.[16]
>
> —CHRISTOPHER HITCHENS

In one concise sentence, Hitchens gives a devastating critique of his understanding of the divine-human drama. As he sees it, God is a detached observer of an experiment, in which weak and sinful humans try to heal themselves. God set up humans for failure, and then, instead of helping them thrive, he condemns them for their weaknesses and mistakes. Unsurprisingly, Hitchens cannot accept a God that would do that!

However, the biblical drama is not as Hitchens imagines. God is not an uninvolved observer of the drama; he has the lead role. Humans are not objects or pawns, but key actors. Humans were created to be well, and when they are not well, God's commands and actions are intended to help them be better.

---

16. Krauss, *Universe from Nothing*, 121.

The Battle within Humanity

> Then the Lord said to Cain, "Why are you angry? Why is your face downcast? If you do what is right, will you not be accepted? But if you do not do what is right, sin is crouching at your door; it desires to have you, but you must rule over it."
>
> —Genesis 4:6–7

After God banished Adam and Eve from the Garden, Eve bore two sons, Cain and Abel. Despite her pain in childbirth, Eve felt blessed by God as she brought new life into the world. Yet jealousy and rage overcame Cain, and he murdered his own brother.

As Genesis progressed, the battle between good and evil played out in the lives of the characters. Adam and Eve were blessed with another son, Seth, who worshipped God. Cain's descendants were violent, but they were clever enough to raise livestock, create music, and forge metal tools.

Noah was a descendant of Seth, a good man in a world that had become corrupt and full of violence. God destroyed the people around Noah in a massive flood, while righteous Noah and his family were saved in an ark God had instructed him to build. Yet when Noah got drunk and shed his clothes, his youngest son disrespected his father, leading Noah to curse his son, even condemning him to be his brothers' slave.

The technology that enabled Cain's descendants to create music and tools, and Noah to build an ark, could also be used for rebellion against God. The people of Babel used technology to build a tower to reach toward the heavens, creating a cultural and religious center without God. Technology, culture, and even religion were infused with both good and evil.

God's Commitment to Make Things Right

> The Lord had said to Abram, "Go from your country, your people and your father's household to the land I will show you. I will make you into a great nation, and I will bless you; I will make your name great, and you will be a blessing. I will bless those who bless you, and whoever curses you I will curse; and all peoples on earth will be blessed through you.
>
> —Genesis 12:1–3

God's plan to renew the world began in the smallest possible way: God chose a man named Abraham, who would be the father of a great nation. God promised to bless Abraham's descendants, with the intention that all peoples on earth would be blessed through them. It was not at all clear how that plan would work, but Abraham and his descendants would play key roles in the divine-human drama.

God committed himself to a covenant relationship with Abraham and his descendants, and he held fast to his covenant promises, even when people did not fulfill their obligations. As decades and centuries passed, God renewed and extended his covenant, adapting it to the circumstances of his chosen people. When the people became slaves in Egypt, he sent Moses to lead them out of Egypt into a land where they could thrive. When they became a nation, God promised to establish a kingdom for David and his descendants that would never end. When they fell into sin, he sent prophets to call them back to his righteous ways of obedience and justice.

Much of the Old Testament is hard to understand from within a modern cultural perspective, but clearly, God was always on the side of good and opposed to evil. He gave the Ten Commandments as a guide to freedom for slaves released from bondage (Exod 20:1), and in the sometimes legalistic rules that followed he gave instructions for promoting hygiene and health, providing for the poor and powerless, and establishing a just society. Later, God established a monarchy in which the king should not oppress his subjects, but uphold God's justice.

God's sacrificial system was unlike the other religions of its time, which attempted to appease or manipulate deities by ritual prostitution, child sacrifice, or self-abuse. Sacrifices provided ways for people to be relieved of guilt and shame, while fellowship offerings and festivals allowed them to celebrate God's goodness and grace.

God had chosen a people, and he was committed to guiding them to a good life. Still, the battle between good and evil continued, and evil sometimes triumphed. Laws became burdensome, religion was perverted, kings became tyrants, and false prophets led people astray.

God's Passionate, Persevering Love

> They broke my covenant, though I was a husband to them," declares the LORD.
>
> —JEREMIAH 31:32

The words used to describe God's role in the biblical drama are shocking: He is like a father, a husband, a nursing mother, a lover, a jilted suitor, even a mother hen. Shocking, because most of the gods people worship are aloof, immune to hurt or rejection.

God's interactions with people in the Old Testament are described in Hebrew words of relationship: *hesed*, the untranslatable word that describes a bond between friends, lovers, and people who need love; *emeth*, faithfulness to relationships, even when grace is required; and *'ahab*, the choice to be joined in a relationship of love and commitment.

Passionate love is jealous—not in a selfish way, but in a protective way. The Old Testament exhibits God's jealous anger and even his wrath. Readers are sometimes shocked to find God getting the attention of his people through illness and plague, military defeat, oppressive kings, or exile to a foreign land. Sometimes, it seems that God allowed evil full rein, to reveal the consequences of evil choices. Still, God's passionate love persisted:

> When Israel was a child, I loved him, and out of Egypt I called my son . . . It was I who taught Ephraim to walk, taking them by the arms; but they did not realize it was I who healed them. I led them with cords of human kindness, with ties of love. To them I was like one who lifts a little child to the cheek, and I bent down to feed them . . . How can I give you up, Ephraim? How can I hand you over, Israel? . . . My heart is changed within me; all my compassion is aroused.[17]

The Battle Rages On

> [Zion's] gates have sunk into the ground;
>
> their bars he has broken and destroyed.
>
> Her king and her princes are exiled among the nations,
>
> the law is no more, and her prophets no
> longer find visions from the LORD.
>
> —LAMENTATIONS 2:9

By the end of the Old Testament era, the outcome of the divine-human drama seemed far from certain. God's chosen people had repeatedly rejected

---

17 Hosea 11:1, 3, 8.

his ways and fallen into sin. Evil had often triumphed over good, and the law, temple worship, and justice had been perverted. Only a small remnant of God's chosen people remained, and they were oppressed by evil forces of politics, war, and religious intrigue.

The outcome of the drama seemed uncertain, until God did something unimaginable.

God Takes to the World Stage

> The Word become flesh and made his dwelling among us.
>
> —JOHN 1:14

God had never been absent from the human drama, but in the person of Jesus Christ he became vulnerable, joining humanity in its struggle against sin and evil.

Jesus was born into a corrupted political and social environment. His parents were forced to flee to Egypt, as jealous King Herod massacred the babies of Bethlehem. The people of his hometown rejected him and tried to push him off a cliff.

He faced evil at every turn. He overcame a frontal attack in the wilderness, where Satan tempted him for forty days. In his three years of ministry, he continually encountered sickness, demonic oppression, and toxic religion. Even his closest friends were not immune to evil influences. He reprimanded his disciples for their power struggles, and when Peter tried to dissuade him from his mission, he said, "Get behind me, Satan." In the end, Satan entered into Judas, one of the twelve disciples, who betrayed him.

At the cross, evil ruled. Jealous and power-hungry Jewish leaders arranged for Jesus to be arrested and brought to an illegal trial in the dead of the night. A Roman governor, who declared Jesus innocent, yielded to pressure and sentenced him to death. Sinners mocked the sinless Son of God as he hung on a cross for their sins. Even a Roman centurion supervising the crucifixion recognized that a righteous man was crucified that day.

As his death approached, Jesus recognized the forces of evil descending upon him, and he said to the authorities coming to arrest him, "This is your hour—when darkness reigns." (Luke 22:52-53)

God through Cosmic Lenses

The Crux of the Drama

Crux [Latin, cross]: A central, pivotal, or decisive point.

The tragedy of the cross is profound and troubling: God the Son dies, and God the Father does not intervene. Evil does its worst, and if it emerges victorious, all hell will break loose. Evil will reign, people will be forever alienated from God, death will be stronger than life, and humanity will be destined for the ash heap.

Why does God allow this to happen? Jesus, the Son of God in human form, represents humanity on the world stage. Evil will do its worst, as the drama reaches its pivotal, decisive point.

Solidarity with Humanity

> God made him who had no sin to be sin for us, so that
> in him we might become the righteousness of God.
>
> —2 CORINTHIANS 5:21

In *Night*, Elie Wiesel's account of the Holocaust, a child is hanged by the Nazis. Wiesel says, "For more than half an hour he stayed there, hanging between life and death . . . his tongue still red, his eyes not yet dazed. Behind I heard a man asking, 'Where is God now?' I heard a voice within me answer him: Where is He? Here He is—He is hanging here on these gallows."[18]

On the cross, Jesus joined humanity in facing the devastating effects of sin and evil.

- Suffering

> Surely he took up our pain and bore our suffering . . .
>
> —ISAIAH 53:4

In his death, Jesus suffered not only physical pain, but also deep mental anguish. He was betrayed by a friend, abandoned by his disciples, mocked by soldiers, whipped until his back was raw, and then forced to carry his own cross until he dropped to the ground in exhaustion. He hung for hours in a desperate position, gasping for each breath, until he finally breathed

---

18. As quoted in Willimon, *Sighing for Eden*, 168.

his last. The pain and mental anguish of the cross placed him in solidarity with all who suffer, either by the actions of others, or in the brokenness of a world oppressed by evil.

- Shame

    Anyone who is hung on a pole is under God's curse.

    —Deuteronomy 21:23

    Jesus ... endured the cross, scorning its shame ...

    —Hebrews 12:2

The cross was not merely a means of execution; it was the most shameful death imaginable, for Jews, Greeks, and Romans. The crucified one hung quite naked for all to see, with nothing to hide his shame and guilt, helpless before the condemnation of bystanders. Jesus shared in the shame of sinful humanity.

- Alienation

    My God, my God, why have you forsaken me?

    —Matthew 27:46

Jesus enjoyed an intimate relationship with his Father, which was the foundation of all that he did as a man. As Jesus hung on the cross, a cloud of separation enveloped him, hiding his Father's face. His anguished cries were not answered, and his Father did nothing to rescue him!

- Death

    The last enemy to be destroyed is death.

    —1 Corinthians 15:26

After a few hours of suffering, Jesus said, "It is finished," took his last breath, and died. Death had triumphed, and the Son of God, in the person of Jesus, was hanging limp and powerless upon the cross!

The misery Jesus endured on the cross was not so remarkable for its intensity; throughout history, people have endured intense suffering. The anguish of Jesus was remarkable because he chose to become a participant in the human tragedy of suffering, pain, shame, alienation, and everything evil in the world.

At the cross, the drama intensifies. Jesus dies, and with his death, all hope of defeating the powers of evil seem to be dead. Will God allow the story to end this way?

The Twist

> You, with the help of wicked men, put Jesus of Nazareth to death by nailing him to the cross. But God raised him from the dead, freeing him from the agony of death, because it was impossible for death to keep its hold on him.
>
> —ACTS 2:23–24

As the tragic drama reached its lowest point, it took an astounding twist: Jesus appeared to his followers, very much alive! He spoke, broke bread, and ate some broiled fish with his disciples

Jesus had told his disciples that he would die and rise from the dead, but they had refused to accept it. When the women found that his tomb was empty, the apostles "did not believe the women, because their words seemed to them as nonsense." Yet they were convinced he was alive, as he appeared to them in the next forty days—one, two, a handful, twelve, even five hundred at one time. Their encounters with the risen Christ Jesus transformed their lives.

Christus Victor

> Having disarmed the powers and authorities, he made a public spectacle of them, triumphing over them by the cross.
>
> —COLOSSIANS 2:15

In Paul's verbal picture, Christ Jesus, a man embodying the fullness of God, enters a coliseum on the world stage. The powers of darkness—sin, death, and a plethora of evil forces—attack from every side. Christ goes down, the forces of evil swarm around him, and the crowd gasps in fear, as evil prevails. Then their hero rises from the dead to vanquish his enemies. He binds them and leads them in a victory parade around the coliseum, while the crowd roars and his followers swarm into the streets of the city.

The victory of the Christ, the Messiah, is a decisive victory for all who identify with him in his death and resurrection. As Heb 2:14–15 says, "Since the children have flesh and blood, he too shared in their humanity so that by his death he might break the power of him who holds the power of death—that is, the devil—and free those who all their lives were held in slavery by their fear of death."

COSMIC IMPACT OF THE CROSS AND RESURRECTION

> Our object . . . is to vindicate the principles of peace and
> justice in the life of the world as against selfish and autocratic
> power . . . The world must be made safe for democracy.[19]
>
> —Woodrow Wilson

World War I was fought mostly in Europe, but it became a world war because other nations believed the war would have a global impact. President Wilson argued that if democracy and justice were not preserved, autocracy and injustice would prevail throughout the world.

The death and resurrection of Jesus took place on the world stage, but they profoundly transformed the entire cosmic order.

- Justice was preserved.

> A non-indignant God would be an accomplice
> in injustice, deception, and violence.[20]
>
> —Miroslav Volf

If a crime is committed and the perpetrator receives little or no punishment, there is a public outcry. Failure of justice undermines cultural foundations of the rule of law, public decency, and protection for victims.

---

19 Library of Congress, "President Woodrow Wilson's Address to Congress, April 2, 1917."

20. Miroslav Volf, *Exclusion and Embrace*, 297, quoted by Rutledge, *Crucifixion*, 131. Volf, a Croatian-born theologian, writes out of his experience in the Balkan conflict of the 1990s, which claimed 130,000 lives.

Instinctively, most people understand that cosmic justice depends upon a power to hold people accountable and balance the scales of justice. But how should God respond to sin and wrong? If he would severely punish the worst offenders, would that preserve justice? Should the person who commits a minor infraction, such as carelessly insulting someone, get off scot-free? The insult might not seem like much, but it could cause great damage to someone in a fragile state of mind.

Strict justice would require that God punish every offender and every offense. That might seem good, but would it be right and just for God to add to the brokenness and pain of humanity by punishing everyone?

At the cross, God's justice was established, as God the Son took upon himself the aggregated sins of all of humanity—past, present, and future.[21] The immensity of the load of sins was matched by the immense stroke of the wrath of God, as the Son bore the just consequences of the sins of all and received the penalty of death. The scale was balanced: On one side was a vast collection of human sins, and on the other side the suffering and death of the infinite, perfect, only-begotten Son of God.

In the mystery of God's plan, cosmic justice was preserved, without the total destruction of sinful humanity. The powers of darkness did not see that coming, as Paul declared, "We declare God's wisdom, a mystery that has been hidden and that God destined for our glory before time began. None of the rulers of this age understood it, for if they had, they would not have crucified the Lord of glory." (1 Cor 2:7–8)

- Mercy triumphed over judgment.[22]

> God presented Christ as a sacrifice of atonement, through the shedding of his blood—to be received by faith. He did this to demonstrate his righteousness ... so as to be just and the one who justifies those who have faith in Jesus.
>
> —ROMANS 3:25–26

---

21. See Isa 53:6.
22. Jas 2:13.

For Us

Nothing would be more satisfying to the powers of darkness than the absolute and eternal punishment of every human offender. God's judgment without mercy would be a failure of his love, and would defeat his purpose in creating humanity for his glory.

How could God's mercy triumph? A common answer is that God should simply forgive everyone. That would not do, for forgiveness without recognizing the offense would empower evil, undermine the foundations of law and morality, and allow the powerful to oppress the weak with impunity.

In 2015, Dylann Roof walked into a Wednesday Bible study at a church in Charleston, South Carolina. The people of that African-American church graciously welcomed him, and he responded by murdering nine of them in cold blood. Amazingly, the people who spoke at his bond hearing offered him forgiveness. Yet forgiveness did not remove the loss and pain of the crime—pain which was borne by the victims. As the daughter of one of the victims said, "You took something very precious from me. I will never talk to her again. I will never, ever, hold her again. But I forgive you. And have mercy on your soul."[23]

Mercy must be more than forgiveness. It must register outrage at the offense, share the pain of the victims, and relinquish a just claim to a penalty. Only the immensity of God's Son suffering for the sins of the world entitles God to offer forgiveness and restoration.

- Righteousness was firmly established.

The cross is not forgiveness pure and simple, but God's
setting aright the world of injustice and deception.[24]

—Miroslav Volf

In a recent year, one of America's cities recorded 812 homicides. Some victims were killed in domestic disputes or fits of anger, while others died from gang violence or drug deals gone bad. Root causes of the violence go much deeper, of course: lack of education or jobs, breakdown of families, decades of racism, and an imperfect criminal justice system. Many of those killed had contributed to the systemic evil of the city, while some victims were simply caught in the crossfire.

23. Berman, "Forgive You."
24. Rutledge, *Crucifixion*, 126.

Some point to just punishment as the solution to violence; civil justice can restrain evil and support moral order. Others emphasize mercy for violent offenders; with drug treatment and education, they might overcome some of the evil forces in their world. Yet a complete solution would be much more radical: sin would need to be eradicated, and evil would need to be overcome. Only by overcoming the powers of darkness could a city be set right.

When Jesus Christ overcame the powers of darkness, the powers of darkness lost their authority and power in the cosmic order. There is no place for sin, evil, or death in the kingdom of God, and in heaven, God's kingdom authority is unchallenged. Yet on the earth, sin and evil are still active, and death claims all flesh. Was Christ's victory incomplete?

World War II ended soon after atomic bombs were dropped on Japanese cities. Yet on a few Pacific islands, fighting and casualties continued for a time. Some resistance fighters did not know that the victors in the war had already been determined, and others refused to accept the outcome.

When Jesus Christ rose from the dead, the outcome of the conflict between God and powers of darkness was clear. Yet the actors on the world stage were left to align themselves with either the dominion of darkness or the kingdom of God.

The Drama Continues

> Now I rejoice in what I am suffering for you, and I fill
> up in my flesh what is still lacking in regard to Christ's
> afflictions, for the sake of his body, which is the church.
>
> —COLOSSIANS 1:24

This is surprising! What could possibly be "lacking" in Christ's afflictions? Jesus Christ had accomplished God's cosmic purpose: Justice was preserved, mercy triumphed, and God's righteous kingdom was established. What could the apostle Paul add to that?

Yet the drama on the world stage did not begin when Jesus was born, and it did not end when Jesus ascended into heaven. The drama spans millennia of human history, with countless saints in meaningful roles. There are Old Testament heroes, faithful parents, reluctant prophets, imperfect kings, and desperate peasants. There are roles in the New Testament for intellectual giants like Paul, as well as humble servants like Tabitha, the woman of Joppa, who was always doing good and helping the poor. There are roles for today's saints as well, as they demonstrate the righteousness of Christ in their personal lives and their life together in the church.

ON EARTH, AS IN HEAVEN

> We continually ask God to fill you with the knowledge of his will
> through all the wisdom and understanding that the Spirit gives,
> so that you may live a life worthy of the Lord and please him
> in every way: bearing fruit in every good work, growing in the
> knowledge of God, being strengthened with all power according
> to his glorious might so that you may have great endurance
> and patience, and giving joyful thanks to the Father, who has
> qualified you to share in the inheritance of his holy people in the
> kingdom of light. For he has rescued us from the dominion of
> darkness and brought us into the kingdom of the Son he loves.
>
> —COLOSSIANS 1:9–13

God's people are no longer under the dominion of the powers of darkness; they obey God and live as children of God. As citizens of God's kingdom, they do good works, grow closer to God, and overcome adversity.

Jesus compared the kingdom of God to yeast, which is hidden in a loaf of bread and has great impact. The kingdom of God is most active in everyday activities: Parents love and train their children, doctors and scientists seek cures for diseases, politicians and police officers and social workers seek justice and human flourishing, and farmers and corporate leaders provide for the needs of the world while protecting the environment. People choose the kingdom of God over the dominion of darkness, taking on difficult challenges and fighting for justice. Every role demonstrates the kingdom of God, for in the life of the kingdom, things are being made right, as they are already right in heaven.

Each person in God's kingdom has a unique role:

A family in our church recently adopted a twelve-year-old child from China. All of their eight children have special needs, requiring time, money, and commitment. The parents believe that God has given them a role in including people in the kingdom of God, sharing with them the benefits of the kingdom.

A pastor in a nearby city moved his family from a safe suburban neighborhood into an inner city neighborhood known for nightly criminal activity. The family is committed to the church he serves there—a church that reflects the kingdom of God by bringing together ex-convicts and college students, former drug addicts and prostitutes, as well as pastoral interns.

A young man I met was arrested and beaten in his native country because of his faith. He had to flee for his life, leaving behind his new wife. After studying in America, he has now returned to his native land to share the good news of Jesus Christ. He has a role in God's kingdom on earth that few others would be able to fill.

My list goes on and on: a young couple lovingly caring for a special needs child, a man persevering after a debilitating stroke, a woman raising children while enduring an illness of continual fatigue, an old friend planning for his role in the kingdom of God after he retires. They are not extras or props on a world stage; they have meaningful roles in God's cosmic drama of overcoming the powers of darkness and bringing into the world the kingdom of the Son.

More

> When you learn that stars, planets, and life disintegrate, and even that consciousness has a finite duration on a cosmological timeline, it can leave you asking, "What is the point of it all?"[1]
>
> —Physicist Brian Greene

An old saint came into my office, bringing with her a young man she had met on her daily walk. He had come from the Netherlands to see his girlfriend and explore writing a book on America's heartland, and since our little crossroads of a town was named Holland, he made a short drive to talk to people of a similar ethnic heritage. He put his recorder on the table between us, and we had an open and honest discussion on a variety of topics. Somehow, we started talking about God and the meaning of life, and I asked what I thought was a rhetorical question: "Is the only purpose of life to have as much fun as you can, and then die?" Without any hesitation, he said, "I think so."

I appreciated his candor, and I didn't know what to say at first. Then I began to talk about people of Dutch heritage, who lived to honor God by loving people, investing in their families, and building healthy communities. Their faith in God gave them a purpose beyond themselves.

Yet I must say that the young man's answer was consistent with his worldview. If nothing lasts forever, investing in people and communities is pointless.

---

1. Porterfield, "I Am Not a Believer in Free Will."

WHERE IS LIFE HEADED?

> One can have the clearest and most complete knowledge of what is, and yet not be able to deduct from that what should be the goal of our human aspirations. Objective knowledge provides us with powerful instruments for the achievement of certain ends, but the ultimate goal itself and the longing to reach it must come from another source.[2]
>
> —Albert Einstein

Views of the future of humanity and the universe fall into four categories:

A Dead End?

> If we live in a universe whose energy is dominated by the energy of nothing, as I have described, the future is indeed bleak. The heavens will become cold and dark and empty . . . Any civilization is guaranteed to disappear in such a universe, starved of energy to survive . . . The future will be dominated by a universe with nothing in it to appreciate its vast mystery.[3]
>
> —Lawrence Krauss

In a best case scenario, civilization will last long enough for the heavens to fade into oblivion. Life on earth will not last that long, since the sun is destined to become a massive red star in about five billion years, swallowing the earth. In fact, the earth will become inhospitable to life long before that. The ultimate future of civilization is bleak.

To avoid facing such a bleak prospect, some speculate that the universe will spawn new universes with new forms of life. Of course, there would be no place for my offspring in any of those new universes.

---

2. Address at Princeton Theological Seminary, May 19, 1939.
3. Krauss, *Universe from Nothing*, 179.

An Evolving Future?

> I think belief in an afterlife is just wishful thinking. There is no reliable evidence for it, and it flies in the face of everything we know in science. I think that when we die we return to dust. But there's a sense in which we live on, in our influence, and in our genes that we pass on to our children.[4]
>
> —STEPHEN HAWKING

If the human future depends upon continuing civilization, humans must adapt to change and create new environments. Hawking believed the earth would support life for only another century or so! Yet he found hope in believing humanity would survive the demise of planet earth, saying, "We will transcend the Earth and learn to exist in space."[5]

Science fiction sagas, such as *Star Trek* and *Star Wars*, envision the possibility of life after the earth becomes uninhabitable. Environmental scientist Andrew J. Rushby describes a future in which "future humans might build interstellar arks, giant ships on which generations of travelers would live and die before delivering colonists to a new destination."[6]

Some who espouse the Participatory Anthropic Principle (PAP, see previous chapter) go even further. Since PAP suggests that reality is generated by information, David Deutsch says, "The process of acquiring knowledge is destined to continue until the end of the universe. And at the end of time, life will have spread throughout space. It will have gained control of all matter and all forces and it will have acquired all the knowledge that there is to know . . . the universe is heading towards something that might be called omniscience."[7]

In such a scenario, life takes more evolved forms, with humanity superseded by artificial intelligence or new forms of life. Humanity fades into the recesses of the evolutionary tree of knowledge.

---

4. Hawking, *Brief Answers*, 38.
5. Hawking, *Brief Answers*, 202.
6. Powell, "How Humans Might Outlive Earth."
7. Redfern, "Anthropic Universe."

God through Cosmic Lenses

A Great Escape?

> When the shadows of this life have gone, I'll fly away.
> Like a bird from prison bars have flown, I'll fly away.
>
> —ALBERT E. BRUMLEY

Written in 1929, "I'll Fly Away" has been called the most-recorded gospel song of all time. Brumley said he got the idea for the song while picking cotton on his father's farm, humming a secular song about escaping from prison.

Adherents of non-Christian religions might also seek escape—from suffering, the illusions of physical life, or an earthbound cycle of death and rebirth. For some, life on earth is a probationary period to be endured on the way to a life of freedom.

Life can be difficult, and the prospect of a better life beyond the universe can give comfort and hope. Yet N.T. Wright points out that, "an escapist or quietest piety" withdraws from engagement with the world, ignores injustice, and does nothing to preserve or enhance life in the natural world.

Life in a New Universe?

> I consider that our present sufferings are not worth comparing with the glory that will be revealed in us. For the creation waits in eager expectation for the children of God to be revealed. For the creation was subjected to frustration [lit. futility], not by its own choice, but by the will of the one who subjected it, in hope that the creation itself will be liberated from its bondage to decay into the freedom of the glory of the children of God. We know that the whole creation has been groaning ... right up to the present time.
>
> —ROMANS 8:18–22

As noted in a previous chapter, the present universe is perfectly suited to the purpose for which God created it. In the universe, the earth was formed, humanity was born, the stage was set for a struggle between good and evil, and the Son of God took human form to win a decisive victory. On the earth, God redeems people to live as his children and enjoy the fruits of a righteous life.

While the universe is an environment of beauty, order, and fertility, it is open to violence, suffering, and death. The apostle Paul describes the universe as "subjected to futility . . . in bondage to decay . . . groaning."

Paul envisions a creation liberated from bondage to decay, suitable for the glorious life of the children of God. Does God plan to renovate the present universe, or will he create something new? If he creates something new, will the new creation be linked to the old, or will the old pass into oblivion?

Imagine living in an old house, with everything falling apart. The plumbing leaks, the lights flicker, and the wind blows through the walls. The carpeting is worn and the floors creak. Termites have gotten into the walls and the foundation is crumbling. Personifying the house, you could say the house is groaning in eager expectation of being set free from decay. Since houses don't have minds, what would you have in mind for the house? You could fix a few things, or even do a major renovation, but the kitchen would still be too small and the closet in the master bedroom entirely inadequate. It might be better to rebuild the house from the ground up, reconstructing the best features of the old house in a new design and better construction. The new house would be like the old, but better.

NEW HEAVEN AND EARTH

> Then I saw "a new heaven and a new earth," for the first heaven
> and the first earth had passed away . . . [and the angel] showed me
> the Holy City, Jerusalem, coming down out of heaven from God.
>
> —REVELATION 21:1, 10

In the pre-scientific language of the first century, "the first heaven and the first earth" referred to the universe, which in John's vision had passed away. Revelation envisions replacement of the universe with "a new heaven and a new earth."

God through Cosmic Lenses

Continuity and Discontinuity

> There must be sufficient continuity to ensure that individuals truly share in the life to come as their resurrected selves and not as new beings given the old names. There must be sufficient discontinuity to ensure that the life to come is free from the suffering and mortality of the old creation.[8]
>
> —John Polkinghorne

If the new creation is similar to the old, will each element of the old creation have a place in the new creation? Will there be lakes and trees, blue skies and beautiful flowers? Will there be houses and pickup trucks? Golf carts and motorcycles? Cuckoo clocks? Old socks and athletic shoes?

Will pets have a place in the new creation? John Polkinghorne says, "I cannot imagine that there will not be animals in the new creation," but he suggests that animals are to be valued "more in the type than in the token."[9]

If parents and spouses are recognizable in the new heaven and earth, how old will they appear? Will they have wrinkles, tattoos, or scars? Will their cute infant faces be reflected in their wizened countenance?

Spiritual Bodies

> So will it be with the resurrection of the dead. The body that is sown is perishable, it is raised imperishable; it is sown in dishonor, it is raised in glory; it is sown in weakness, it is raised in power; it is sown a natural body, it is raised a spiritual body . . . And just as we have borne the image of the earthly man [Adam], so shall we bear the image of the heavenly man [Jesus]. I declare to you, brothers and sisters, that flesh and blood cannot inherit the kingdom of God, nor does the perishable inherit the imperishable.
>
> —1 Corinthians 15:42–50

What form or substance will people have in their eternal home? Will they be ephemeral ghosts? Will their "souls"—their essence—somehow continue to exist in a disembodied state? Will they have physical bodies, in the

---

8. Polkinghorne, *Exploring Reality*, 152–53.
9. Polkinghorne, *Science and the Trinity*, 152.

form of matter from the universe? Will their bodies be comprised of some other unknown material?

Paul says that those who live eternally with God will have "spiritual bodies." Although it is common to think of spiritual as less real than physical, the opposite is true. Paul says a spiritual body is imperishable, glorious, and powerful.

In *The Great Divorce*, C.S. Lewis imagines glorified people with spiritual bodies, who act as guides for ghosts on the outskirts of heaven. The narrator calls them "the solid people," in contrast to those like himself, "the shadowy company" of those not yet glorified. He says, "I saw people coming to meet us . . . The earth shook under their tread as their strong feet sunk into the wet turf . . . [For me] walking proved difficult. The grass, hard as diamonds to my unsubstantial feet, made me feel as if I were walking on wrinkled rock."

The prototype of resurrected spiritual bodies is the resurrected body of Jesus. When Jesus rose from the dead, his physical body did not remain as a relic in the tomb; his body was transformed into a more substantial spiritual body. Jesus was recognizable in his spiritual body, because the essence of his physical body was integrated into his spiritual body.

In his spiritual body, Jesus ate bread with the disciples. When he put bread or fish in his mouth, it disappeared from view. Yet when the disciples were in a room with the door closed and locked, he passed through the wall as if it were merely a hologram.

The Fullness of God's Presence

> Then I saw "a new heaven and a new earth," for the first heaven and the first earth had passed away . . . And I heard a loud voice from the throne saying, "Look! God's dwelling place is now among the people, and he will dwell with them. They will be his people, and God himself will be with them and be their God.
>
> —REVELATION 21:1–3

In the biblical worldview, God reigns in heaven. (Heaven in this usage is separate from the created universe, which is denoted as "heaven and earth.") Yet God is not restricted to heaven; he is also present and active on earth.

Old Testament people rarely sensed God's presence on earth. Jacob had a dream of angels ascending and descending a stairway to heaven, and he said, "Surely the Lord is in this place, and I was not aware of it." Moses went up on the mountain of God, and God spoke directly to him, giving him the law. The Israelites understood that God's glory was ensconced in the tabernacle (and later the temple).

God was present in the person of Jesus. John 1:14 says, "The Word became flesh and made his dwelling (lit., "tabernacled") among us. We have seen his glory, the glory of the one and only Son, who came from the Father, full of grace and truth." Matthew saw in Jesus a fulfillment of Isaiah's promise of a child, Immanuel, meaning in Hebrew, "God with us."

After Jesus ascended to heaven, God came to his people through the Holy Spirit. Yet even the most pious saints desire more of God's presence.

In the new heaven and the new earth, God himself will be continually with his people. No temple will be needed in the new Jerusalem, "because the Lord Almighty and the Lamb are its temple" (Rev 21:22).

Life Made Right

> He will wipe every tear from their eyes. There will
> be no more death or mourning or crying or pain,
> for the old order of things has passed away.
>
> —REVELATION 21:4

In the new creation, life is *right*. The "old order"—the frustration and decay that characterizes life on earth—passes away, to allow God's children to live without pain, tears, or death.

For that to happen, everything in the new creation must also be transformed and made right. Revelation echoes a vision of a new universe in Isa 65:17–25, where "the wolf and the lamb will feed together, and the lion will eat straw like the ox . . . They will neither harm nor destroy on all my holy mountain."

LIVING IN LIGHT OF ETERNITY

> The heavens will disappear with a roar; the elements will be
> destroyed by fire, and the earth and everything done in it will
> be laid bare. Since everything will be destroyed in this way,
> what kind of people ought you to be? You ought to live holy

> and godly lives as you look forward to the day of God and speed its coming. That day will bring about the destruction of the heavens by fire, and the elements will melt in the heat. But in keeping with his promise we are looking forward to a new heaven and a new earth, where righteousness dwells. So then, dear friends, since you are looking forward to this, make every effort to be found spotless, blameless and at peace with him.
>
> —2 PETER 3:10–14

Peter could not be clearer: The physical universe of space, time and matter will be destroyed, to be replaced by "a new heaven and a new earth."

Yet the transitory nature of the universe does not make human life insignificant. In fact, it gives greater urgency to life in the present, for it is in the present that people get right with God, "spotless, blameless, and at peace with God."

Every aspect of life is transformed by the hope of eternal righteousness with God.

Already Living in Eternity

> Happy is the man who can recognize in the work of To-day a connected portion of the work of life, and an embodiment of the work of Eternity. The foundations of his confidence are unchangeable, for he has been made a partaker of Infinity. He strenuously works out his daily enterprises, because the present is given him for a possession . . . [He is] not slighting his temporal existence, remembering that in it only is individual action possible, nor yet shutting out from his view that which is eternal, knowing that Time is a mystery which man cannot endure to contemplate until eternal Truth enlighten it."[10]
>
> —JAMES CLERK MAXWELL

Maxwell understood that the finite realm of temporal existence is not a precursor to eternity, but a part of it. Life can only be lived in the present, but the present is a slice of eternity.

---

10 Glazebrook, *James Clerk Maxwell and Modern Physics*, 39-40.

Maxwell strenuously invested in his work, because he saw it as part of his eternal purpose, given by God. His work has endured into the present day, in four elegant equations describing the relationship of electricity and magnetism. Does his work also live on in the new heaven and earth?

Work with Lasting Value

> What you do in the present—by painting, preaching, singing, sewing, praying, teaching, building hospitals, digging wells, campaigning for justice, writing poems, caring for the needy, loving your neighbor as yourself—will last into God's future.[11]
>
> —N.T. Wright

Like Maxwell, Wright is anxious to affirm the value of human activity in the present, and he suggests that human actions and creations in the current universe will be preserved in a redeemed earth. As an example, he says, "I don't know what musical instruments we shall have to play Bach in God's new world, though I'm sure Bach's music will be there." (I wonder whether the choirs of heaven will take time to sing *Jesus Loves Me*, or rejoice with an out-of-tune praise song composed by a four-year-old child.)

Theologian J. Todd Billings points to the difficulty in deciding what will "last into God's future." Will the work of an auto mechanic last when automobiles are unnecessary? Will the work of deer hunters have a place in the new creation, where "they will neither harm nor destroy in all my holy mountain?"[12] Will the work of garbage collectors or oil rig workers "last into God's future?"

Jesus said in Luke 12:33, "Sell your possessions and give to the poor. Provide purses for yourselves that will not wear out, a treasure in heaven that will never fail, where no thief comes near and no moth destroys." He was not referring to treasure in the new heaven and earth, as if gold could be sent on ahead, but treasure with God. In a similar parable in Luke 12, Jesus speaks of being "rich toward God."

The lasting value of work is not the work itself, but the faithfulness of the worker. In the parable of ten minas in Luke 19:17, the master says, "Well done, my good servant! Because you have been trustworthy in a very small matter, take charge of ten cities."

---

11. Wright, *Surprised by Hope*, 193.
12. Billings, "New View of Heaven."

More

Because God entrusts opportunities to his faithful servants, their work matters. The gardener or environmental scientist cares for God's creation, to hear God say, "Well done, good and faithful servant." The musician creates music, not to last for eternity, but for the glory of God. The medical researcher develops cures for diseases that will not exist in the new creation, because God is pleased when people are healed.

Worship: Anticipating God's Presence

As the church withdraws from everyday life to worship, the life of the future invades the present: Sins are forgiven, hearts purified, and relationships restored. All who observe will echo 1 Cor 14:25, saying, "God is really among you."

Yet worship does not end at the door of a church building. God can be present as a believer goes into a hospital, a classroom, or a busy office. His glory can be seen on a walk in the woods, or through an electron microscope in a biophysics laboratory. The Holy Spirit is active in the faithful love of a husband and wife or impassioned advocacy for justice.

Relationships Made Right

> Since, then, you have been raised with Christ, set your hearts on things above, where Christ is, seated at the right hand of God. Set your minds on things above, not on earthly things. For you died, and your life is now hidden with Christ in God. When Christ, who is your life, appears, then you also will appear with him in glory. Put to death, therefore, whatever belongs to your earthly nature: sexual immorality, impurity, lust, evil desires and greed, which is idolatry . . . as God's chosen people, holy and dearly loved, clothe yourselves with compassion, kindness, humility, gentleness and patience. Bear with each other and forgive one another if any of you has a grievance against someone. Forgive as the Lord forgave you. And over all these virtues put on love, which binds them all together in perfect unity.
>
> —COLOSSIANS 3:1–14

God through Cosmic Lenses

Among the greatest joys of eternal life in paradise will be rich relationships, redeemed and made right. Imagine a life with glorious people, each faultless and beautiful in your eyes. Imagine a world of righteous relationship, where men and women enrich each other's lives without fear or shame. Imagine a world of kindness, humility and gentleness, with each person seeking the best for everyone. Imagine a world of perfect love, where the warmth of God's love is reflected in every face and every word.

Paul invites his readers to set their hearts on the life to come, which is assured by the resurrection of Jesus Christ and his ascension to glory and authority over all things. A glorious life awaits. But why wait until life on earth is over? Paul instructs his readers to fix their earthly relationships. They can eradicate sinful, destructive behaviors. They can heal broken relationships by graciousness and forgiveness. They can come together in love, kindness, and gentleness, tasting the life of heaven.

Jesus Christ over All

> [God] made known to us the mystery of his will according to his good pleasure, which he purposed in Christ, to be put into effect when the times reach their fulfillment—to bring unity to all things in heaven and on earth under Christ.
>
> —EPHESIANS 1:9–10

In the new creation, God will be with his people. Jesus Christ will reign as Lord and King, and God's people will live in righteousness, peace and joy.

Jesus brought the kingdom of God to earth. As he began his ministry, he declared, "The time has come. The kingdom of God has come near." He sent out his disciples to heal the sick and declare that the kingdom of God was near. Yet it was incomplete, as Jesus instructed his disciples to pray, "Your kingdom come, your will be done, on earth as it is in heaven."

In the new heaven and earth, the reign of God will be complete. Christ will rule over all things, and all things will be brought together as they should be.

More

A FUTURE AND A HOPE

> The things that began to happen after that were so great and beautiful that I cannot write them down. And for us this is the end of all the stories, and we can most truly say that they all lived happily ever after. But for them it was only the beginning of the real story. All their life in this world and all their adventures in Narnia had only been the title and the cover page: now at last they were beginning Chapter One of the Great Story, which no one on earth has read: which goes on forever: in which every chapter is better than the one before.[13]
>
> —C.S. Lewis, *The Last Battle*

The story of our lives begins on a small planet in an unimaginably large universe. It is a real story, and everything we do contributes to our story—and the entire Story, God's Story.

Yet the Story, and our personal stories, will not end when we die or when the universe passes into oblivion. When life on earth is done, we will find that we have been characters in a grand and glorious Story, which goes on forever, as Jesus Christ reigns to make all things right.

---

13 Lewis, *Last Battle*, 183–84.

Bibliography

Abbott, Edwin Abbott. *Flatland: A Romance of Many Dimensions.* Oxford: Oxford World Classics, 2006.
Alexander, Eban. "Proof of Heaven: A Doctor's Experience of the Afterlife." *Newsweek*, October 8, 2012.
Baxter, Richard. "The Divine Life. Part I: The Knowledge of God." In *The Practical Works of the Reverend Richard Baxter, and a Critical Examination of his Writings*, vol. 13, edited by William Orme, 28–34. London: James Duncan, 1830.
Berman, Mark. "I Forgive You." *The Washington Post*, June 19, 2015.
Billings, J. Todd. "The New View of Heaven Is Too Small." *Christianity Today*, February 15, 2018. https://www.christianitytoday.com/ct/2018/february-web-only/new-view-of-heaven-too-small-resurrection-hope.html.
Boyle, Robert. "Of the High Veneration Man's Intellect Owes to God." In *The Works of Robert Boyle*, edited by Ted Davis, 172. Vol. 10. London: Pickering and Chatto, 2000.
Collins, Francis S. *The Language of God: A Scientist Presents Evidence for Belief.* New York: Simon and Schuster, 2006.
Cross, F.L. and E.A. Livingstone, eds. *The Oxford Dictionary of the Christian Church.* 3rd edition. Oxford: Oxford University Press, 1997.
Darwin, Charles. *On the Origin of Species by Means of Natural Selection.* London: Dover, 2006.
Davies, Paul. *Cosmic Jackpot: Why Our Universe Is Just Right for Life.* Boston: Mariner, 2007.
Dirac, Paul. "Evolution of the Physicist's Picture of Nature." *Scientific American*, May, 1963.
Dizikes, Peter. "When the Butterly Effect Took Flight." *MIT News Magazine*, February 22, 2011.
Dostoevsky, Fyodor. *The Brothers Karamazov.* Translated by Constance Garnett. New York: Modern Library, 1996.
Drummond, Henry. *The Lowell Lectures on the Ascent of Man.* London: Hodder and Stoughton, 1896.
D'Souza, Dinesh. *What's So Great about God: A Reasonable Defense of the Goodness of God in a World Filled with Suffering.* Carol Stream, IL: Tyndale, 2013.
Dukas, Helen and Banesh Hoffman. *Albert Einstein: The Human Side.* Princeton: Princeton University Press, 1979.

Bibliography

Dyson, Freeman. *Disturbing the Universe.* New York: Harper and Row, 1979.

Einstein, Albert. "On a Heuristic View Concerning the Production and Transformation of Light." In *The Collected Papers of Albert Einstein, Volume 2: The Swiss Years: Writings 1900-1909*, edited by John Stachel, David C. Cassidy, Jürgen Renn, and Robert Schulmann. Princeton: Princeton University Press, 1990.

Einstein, Albert and Leopold Infeld. *Evolution of Physics from Early Concepts to Relativity and Quanta.* New York: Simon and Schuster, 1938.

Feynman, Richard P. *The Feynman Lectures on Physics. Vol. 3.* Pasadena, CA: California Institute of Technology, 1965.

———. *The Meaning of It All: Thoughts of a Citizen-Scientist.* Reading, MA: Perseus, 1998

Feynman, Richard Phillips and Ralph Leighton. *Surely You're Joking, Mr. Feynman!* New York: W.W. Norton, 1985.

Galli, Mark and Ted Olsen, *131 Christians Everyone Should Know.* Nashville: Broadman and Holman, 2000.

Glazebrook, Richard. *James Clerk Maxwell and Modern Physics.* New York: Macmillan and Co., 1896.

Gleick, James. *Genius: The Life and Science of Richard Feynman.* New York: Pantheon, 1992.

Gleiser, Marcelo. "The Origin of the Universe: From Nothing Everything?" *NPR*, March 27, 2013. www.npr.org/sections/13.7/2013/03/26/175352714/the-origin-of-the-universe-from-nothing-everything.

Greene, Brian. "How the Higgs Boson Was Found." *Smithsonian Magazine*, July 2013.

Grudem, Wayne. *Systematic Theology: An Introduction to Biblical Doctrine.* Grand Rapids: Zondervan, 1994.

Hawking, Stephen. *Brief Answers to the Big Questions.* New York: Bantam, 2018.

———. "Does God Play Dice?" https://www.hawking.org.uk/in-words/lectures/does-god-play-dice.

Hawking, Stephen and Leonard Mlodinov. *The Grand Design.* New York: Bantam, 2010.

Hobson, Art. "There are no particles, there are only fields," *American Journal of Physics* 81 (2013) 211–23.

Larsen, Timothy. "War Is Over, If You Want It: Beyond the Conflict between Faith and Science." *Perspectives on Science and Christian Faith* 60.3 (2008) 147–55.

Hoefer, Carl. "Causal Determinism." *The Stanford Encyclopedia of Philosophy.* https://plato.stanford.edu/archives/spr2016/entries/determinism-causal/.

Hunter, Archibald Macbride. *Jesus, Lord and Saviour.* Grand Rapids: Eerdmans, 1978.

Hutchinson, Ian. "James Clerk Maxwell and the Christian Proposition." *MIT IAP Seminar: The Faith of Great Scientists*, Jan 1998, 2006. http://silas.psfc.mit.edu/Maxwell/.

Isaacson, Walter. *Einstein: His Life and Universe.* New York: Simon & Schuster, 2008.

Kaiser, Christopher. "A Scientist's View of the Universe." *Crux* 15 (1979) 162–71.

Kidner, Derek. *Genesis: An Introduction and Commentary.* Downers Grove: InterVarsity, 1975.

Kilmer, Joyce. "Trees." *Poetry* 2 (1913) 160.

Krauss, Lawrence. *A Universe from Nothing.* Free Press, 2012.

———. "Unlikely." *Does the Universe Have a Purpose? A Templeton Conversation.* https://quantumguru.files.wordpress.com/2013/04/161.pdf

Lawson, Robert W. and Albert Einstein. *Relativity: The Special and the General Theory.* United States: Crown Trade Paperbacks, 1961.

Lewis, C.S. *Mere Christianity.* New York: Macmillan, 1958.

———. *Miracles: A Preliminary Study.* New York: Macmillan, 1947.

Bibliography

———. "Is Theology Poetry?" *The Weight of Glory: And Other Addresses*. New York: HarperOne, 2001.

———. "Religion and Science." *God in the Dock: Essays on Theology and Ethics*, edited by Walter Hooper, 72–75. Grand Rapids: Eerdmans, 1970.

———. *Surprised by Joy*. New York: Harcourt, Brace and World, 1955.

Mander, William. "Pantheism." *The Stanford Encyclopedia of Philosophy*. http://plato.stanford.edu/archives/sum2013/entries/pantheism/.

Mastin, Luke. "Bertrand Russell and Alfred North Whitehead." *Story of Mathematics*. http://www.storyofmathematics.com/20th_russell.html.

Meynell, Mark. *A Wilderness of Mirrors*. Grand Rapids: Zondervan, 2015.

Michelson, A.A. *Annual Register 1894–1895*. University of Chicago. https://babel.hathitrust.org/cgi/pt?id=njp.32101065108746&view=1up&seq=166&q1=Michelson.

Miele, Frank. "Darwin's Dangerous Disciple: An Interview with Richard Dawkins." *Skeptic Magazine*. https://scepsis.net/eng/articles/id_3.php.

Moore, Ruth. *Niels Bohr: The Man, His Science, and the World They Changed*. New York: Knopf, 1966.

Myers, David G. *A Friendly Letter to Skeptics and Atheists*. San Francisco: Jossey-Bass, 2008.

Nilsson, Jeff. "Albert Einstein: Imagination is more important than knowledge." *The Saturday Evening Post*, March 20, 2010. https://www.saturdayeveningpost.com/2010/03/imagination-important-knowledge/.

O'Neill, John, ed. *Freud and the Passions*. University Park, PA: Penn State University Press, 1996.

Orwell, George. *Animal Farm*. London: Harcourt, Brace, and Co., 1954.

Pelikan, Jaroslav. *The Emergence of the Catholic Tradition (100–600)*. Chicago: University of Chicago Press, 1971.

Phillips, J.B. *Your God Is Too Small*. New York: Macmillan, 1960.

Plato. *Five Dialogues by Plato*. Translated by Benjamin Jowett. London: Philosophy Classics, 2018.

Polkinghorne, John. "The Anthropic Principle and the Science and Religion Debate." *Faraday Paper* 4 (2007) 1–4. www.faraday.cam.ac.uk/wp-content/uploads/resources/Faraday%20Papers/Faraday%20Paper%204%20Polkinghorne_EN.pdf

———. *Exploring Reality: The Intertwining of Science and Religion*. New Haven: Yale University Press, 2005.

———. *Quantum Theory: A Very Short Introduction*. New York: Oxford University Press, 2002.

———. *Science and the Trinity: The Christian Encounter with Reality*. New Haven: Yale University Press, 2004.

———. "Scripture and an Evolving Creation." *Science and Christian Belief* 21.2 (2009) 163–73.

Porterfield, Dan. "I am Not a Believer in Free Will: A conversation with Brian Greene." *Forbes*, July 21, 2020. Forbes.com/sites.dporterfield/2020/07/21.

Powell, Corey S. "How Humans Might Outlive Earth, the Sun . . . and Even the Universe." *NBC News*, Dec. 20, 2017.

Randall, Lisa. *Knocking on Heaven's Door*. New York: Harper Collins, 2011.

———. "Theories of the Brane." *Edge*. www.edge.org/conversation/lisa_randall-theories-of-the-brane-lisa-randall.

Bibliography

Redfern, Martin. "The Anthropic Universe." Australian Broadcasting Commission: *The Science Show*, February 18, 2006. https://www.abc.net.au/radionational/programs/scienceshow/the-anthropic-universe/3384520.

Rutledge, Fleming. *The Crucifixion: Understanding the Death of Jesus Christ*. Grand Rapids: Eerdmans, 2015.

Sagan, Carl. *The Cosmic Connection: An Extraterrestrial Perspective*. New York: Doubleday, 1973.

Shakespeare, William. *As You Like It*. Edited by Michael Hattaway. Cambridge: Cambridge University Press, 2000.

Sykes, Christopher, ed. *No Ordinary Genius: The Illustrated Richard Feynman*. New York: Norton, 1994.

University of California Museum of Paleontology. "William Paley." https://ucmp.berkeley.edu/history/paley.html#:~:text=The%20hinges%20in%20the%20wings,distraction%20of%20thought%20by%20variety.

Viney, Donald. "Process Theism," *The Stanford Encyclopedia of Philosophy*. https://plato.stanford.edu/archives/sum2020/entries/process-theism/.

Weinberg, Steven. "A Designer Universe?" *The New York Review of Books*, October 21, 1999.

Whitman, Walt. *Leaves of Grass*. London: Penguin, 1986.

Willimon, William H. *Sighing for Eden*. Nashville: Abingdon, 1985.

Wilson, Woodrow. "President Woodrow Wilson's Address to Congress, April 2, 1917." Washington, D.C.: Library of Congress, 1917.

Wright, N.T. *Simply Christian: Why Christianity Makes Sense*. San Francisco: Harper, 2006.

Yancey, Philip. "The Paradox of Great Price." *Christianity Today*, December 17, 1982.

———. *Reaching for the Invisible God: What Can We Expect to Find?* Grand Rapids: Zondervan, 2000.

www.ingramcontent.com/pod-product-compliance
Lightning Source LLC
Chambersburg PA
CBHW051934160426

43198CB00013B/2152